Think
Yourself
RESILIENT

Think
Yourself
RESILIENT

Harness Your Emotions.
Build Your Confidence.
Transform Your Life.

James Elliott

THREAD

Published by Thread in 2023

An imprint of Storyfire Ltd.
Carmelite House
50 Victoria Embankment
London EC4Y 0DZ

www.thread-books.com

This book draws on the author's experience to identify strategies
that could help avoid mental health crises. It is not intended to
replace professional help – counselling, pharmaceuticals,
or other therapies – where that is needed.

ISBN: 978-1-80314-607-2
eBook ISBN: 978-1-80314-606-5

This book is for Georgina.
My daughter, my love, you are my greatest gift.

CONTENTS

PREFACE

When my editor asked me to write this preface, I really didn't know what to put in it. I don't think I had ever read a preface to a book before, not all of it at least. I thought it was just this thing you skip past when you start a book so you can feel good about already being on page 10. I've since been told that a preface can be a relatively short text that explains why the author wrote the book. It's supposed to give the reader some context and background about the author and is meant to help them engage with the book.

Due to various circumstances that will I hope become apparent in this book, I only started reading properly when I was in my mid-twenties. I don't think my favourite childhood book, *The Hungry Caterpillar*, had a preface and I don't remember if any of the books I read up to my mid-twenties had a preface either.

Now, like most people, I skip past the preface. But really this is like failing to read the instructions before assembling a flat pack. We dismiss this step and try to work it out. But in hindsight, the instructions might actually prove useful, considering how many bookcases can't hold the weight of any books, how many beds are unsuitable to sleep in, and how many times I have woken with a start in the night because my wardrobe has imploded.

*

I joined the British Army in 2006 when I was 18 years old and went into the famous Airborne Forces. I served in the Airborne as a paratrooper with great pride, until I decided to leave in 2020.

This book is not a war story, however. I am sorry to disappoint, but I have no stories to tell. At least, if I do, there is very little I feel personally comfortable to talk about, because my experiences were either really sad and tragic, or really boring. Presenting this as a war memoir would make for either a very embellished or incredibly dull read.

Before I joined the Army, things were not great. I was born in Hammersmith, London, and grew up on a council estate in a small town called Witney in Oxfordshire. I despised school and despite showing some promise, I was a deeply sad and traumatised child.

I knew this in my heart at the time, but what 13-year-old has the language skills to explain that their drug-dealing father was an incredibly intimidating, awful and violent man? I was struggling far too much with my mental health to perform at school and found myself very quickly working on building sites, paid cash in hand, mainly carrying bags of dry plaster and making brews.

As I got older, I began to take more drugs and found myself very quickly surrounded by the wrong people. I revelled in the perception of power that I thought being part of this bad crowd gave me. It felt validating to be known as that one guy people could turn to for drugs or connections to get drugs.

I knew things had fallen into a deep state of desperation whenever I would retell stories from my childhood as if I was proud of my biological father and his behaviour, which included fights and intimidation. He went to prison when I was 13. His drug racket was estimated to be worth £2 million when he was caught, with 100 kg of cannabis (and he admitted to have smuggled more than 500 kg into the UK). His safety deposit boxes contained stashes of cash, coke, cannabis and floppy disks (remember them?!). He was one of those men who idolise the idea of being a drug dealer. I think he wanted to be like the characters he looked up to in movies like *The Godfather*, *Goodfellas* and *Scarface*, all regularly playing in our house, because those movies show the status, power and influence that supposedly come with drug dealing.

Let me assure you, the reality was quite different. A wife who's terrified of you, hiding herself underneath her son's bed to avoid being beaten by her raging drugged husband. Taking so many drugs your son finds you passed out on the couch, and you don't wake up even after he pulls your eyelids open. Screaming and shouting constantly. Kicking your son through the kitchen. Being violent at every opportunity. All so you can walk into a restaurant and the head waiter recognises you from your 'reputation' and finds a table for you. It's a really awful way to live your life. It also damages everyone around you, and I realised I needed to do something about that.

The bad experiences of my childhood, of course, came through in my adolescence. I was lost and angry. It ended up drawing me to the British Army, because I felt that would offer me the things I was missing – unity, a tribe, friendships, purpose, direction, consistency, routine, discipline, and validation from an authority figure. These were all things that by the age of 18 I needed and desperately craved, and which made me vulnerable.

The Army is an incredible institution for taking vulnerable boys and helping them grow into something more. While in the British Armed Forces, I served in Afghanistan, attempted Special Forces selection and failed, and earned my parachute wings. I learned huge amounts about human behaviour. I was witness to the extremities of behaviours through high-pressure situations, while also building strong bonds with the soldiers around me, who I'm proud to call friends to this day. They are probably the best part about me: funny, ridiculous, brilliant and guiding – both in showing me what I should be doing, and what I should definitely not be doing.

*

In 2016 I was struggling with poor mental health. As a result of this, several of my relationships broke down. I had outbursts of damaging and irrational behaviour that those on the receiving end had every right to hold against me. I found myself imploding, being moody and unapproachable. I became reckless after drinking – dangerously so – not caring about who I would hurt or offend, speaking and acting aggressively and inappropriately towards people who did not deserve such abuse. I was starting to slip back into becoming my biological father, building an identity on being aggressive, arrogant and vile to such a degree that I was increasingly ashamed of the person I was becoming.

At this time, I was also a strength and conditioning coach at Colchester Rugby Club. It was the mentoring side of this job that ignited my love for helping others.

It was during this time that I came to the sudden realisation that my experience of poverty had deeply affected me in life. My mum had nothing and when my biological dad went to prison, it became painfully apparent that we were a struggling family, living in social housing. I have to add a caveat here, though, that my step-dad, who I actually called 'Dad' and who joined our family later on, worked himself to the bone to provide for us. He's a straight-up, decent man. I mean, how do you even begin to quantify taking on that much emotional baggage? What a guy.

*

The realisation of my childhood trauma came to me when I was afforded some breathing space in October 2016, as I found myself at RAF Brize Norton as part of the British Army's Army Parachute Jumping Instructors platoon. We would teach low-level parachuting (the type of parachuting done by the Airborne Forces) to young soldiers and those in need of a refresher course. It was incredible, and there was a glaringly obvious link between this and the sports psychology training I had done with the rugby team in Colchester.

Very soon I found myself writing to the head of mental health delivery in the British Army, saying that I thought we weren't proactive enough when it came to soldiers' mental health and that we should be teaching mental resilience from the start. Proactive measures prevent mental health breakdowns later on, and prevention is much better than waiting until people are sitting on the floor in their shower, fully clothed and shaking, screaming into their hands and feeling helpless.

Army headquarters agreed, and before I knew it I was out of the parachute training school and busy creating and delivering a fantastic course on mental resilience that we called the Mental Resilience Training Programme. This was the first of its kind in the British military, and I delivered it to regiments of soldiers in the south of the country, including Special Forces operators preparing for challenging deployments. I truly found running this course to be a really powerful calling, and I enjoyed it immensely. It was during this time that my academic journey began, and I quickly fell in love with studying. It started with a simple suicide awareness course, which led to courses on sports psychology, counselling, advanced psychology, advanced cognitive behaviour therapy (CBT), my accreditation as a psychotherapist and to where I am now, working on my master's degree in war and psychiatry.

However, there was a massive spanner in the works as there was no career development beyond this course, and I found myself stuck in rank and position, running the risk of serious detriment to my pension. I decided to terminate my contract with the British Army in January 2020.

I continued where I'd left off with my studies and became accredited as a psychotherapist in 2020. In the years that followed, I delivered mental resilience training and worked with Paralympians, the NHS, the Scottish Police, the Liberal Democratic Party, Thames Valley Police and the Fire Service. I worked with St Joseph's Rugby Academy, with many talented, high-performing rugby athletes, and with soldiers, athletes and business people. I have trained people from all walks of life, with different backgrounds and needs. Once I qualified as a psychotherapist I also started one-on-one therapy and counselling. I wrote for magazines and started growing my social media presence. I started my master's degree at King's College London in war and psychiatry. And finally, I was approached about writing a book. (I also have five world records, three of them Guinness World Records, but more on that later!)

My life has changed drastically and for the better. Most importantly of all, I have developed a close and loving relationship with my daughter. I see her almost every day during term time, and it's wonderful. The satisfaction of knowing that I have the capability and have actively made the choice to never expose my daughter to the same experiences and environment that I was exposed to, brings me so much joy. I see my close friends a lot more too, and just generally I feel very loved and happy. I wouldn't be where I am now without the people in my life. I'm actually close to believing there is no such thing as 'self-made'. I would still be on the bottom rung of the ladder if my friends hadn't rallied around me and helped me out. In that sense, a life is less like a soliloquy and more like a movie poster with you as the protagonist and your friends playing the other big parts that make up the cast and influence the outcome of the film. After all, it wouldn't be much of a movie if you were just on your own.

I managed to turn those experiences from something awful that happened to me into something that has happened *for* me, and that I've been able to use to build my mental resilience. This has been the key in finding the motivation for what I do, and for writing this book.

There is always nuance and subjectivity to everything we experience. Some of it we get to process, and some of it we get to explore further. What I have discovered is that studying and learning from the things that happen to us gives them meaning and brings us closer to discovering who we truly are. You can take the things that happen to you, and the emotional challenges that you face, and use them as learning points.

This is a book about how we can use key psychological skills to develop our mental resilience. We can use them to instil a level of control in our lives, creating comfort and confidence. Instead of resigning ourselves to 'it is what it is', we can evolve this to 'it is what I choose to make it'. This is a book about learning how to stop fearing adversity and challenge in your life, and instead use them to your advantage to forge a resilient mindset. From the pursuit of greatness to the tragedies we face every day, this book will, I hope, show you the brilliance of the total human experience and how you can have faith in your ability to handle it. It's written through observation and practice, from both my professional and my personal life.

Now, let us turn surviving into thriving.

INTRODUCTION

Rock bottom

I have never felt this awful before in my life. My brain feels as if it has swelled in my head from the heat and has ceased to function properly. If I turn my head to the left or right, it feels as if there is a split-second delay and my brain swivels round in my skull. I can't even string a sentence together in my thoughts anymore. All reasoning and logic have gone, and I am slowly slipping into a state of panic.

I am on the infamous marches in the mountains of Brecon Beacons, going through the selection course for the British Special Air Services (SAS). The bergan on my back has gone from a seemingly manageable load to the approximate weight of the moon. My lower back has seized up, and I can no longer feel my legs, apart from the blisters, a large one on each heel (despite the huge amounts of zinc oxide tape and Compeeds) and several between each toe. Normally, such discomforts wouldn't phase me. I have been serving in the British Airborne Forces for nearly six years by this point. I am a young soldier, just 24 years old, fit and extremely motivated. I am competent with a map and compass, and I am in a good place: I feel prepared, trained, fit and confident in my abilities. But the heat, my god the heat, it has drained the life from me. I'm six hours into a hot June day, continually going up and down mountains, never knowing which checkpoint could be my last. All I know is that I have to keep going. That's the truth of the Special Forces selection. Forget what you see on TV, nobody shouts at you – that is what basic training and training courses are for. During selection, you are not shouted at, which actually makes it harder. No member of staff is going to tell you that you have been moving too slowly and no one will make the time to assess each march: they expect you to know that you haven't been moving fast enough and to hurry yourself up. Six hours into this day, and after weeks of this, I am spent. I'll soon run out of water and food, but at this point this feels irrelevant, because whatever I put in my mouth comes out the other end in quick time. It's bloody awful.

Despite all this pain, all I can think in this moment is how I will never give up. I will move my left foot and then my right foot for as long as it takes, and inevitably, the rest of my body will follow. I just have to keep moving forward, keep pushing and get to the next checkpoint. The number of soldiers in the selection has dwindled right down, but I feel confident that I will pass this phase.

This morning is different though. I have done everything I normally do. I have checked my tape, my kit, my boots, my food, my water. Everything was correct and in the right place, but as the morning sun creeps up, I know today will be a scorcher. The last few days have been unbearably hot, and more than once I have found myself falling over my own feet, dizzy and clumsy, struck by the heat. Today's heat is on another level, and when I was sitting in the back of the transport on the way to the start point I knew it would be almost unbearable. I try to focus on other things, anything else but the debilitating heat.

I believe that my mindset has always been solid. I have high self-efficacy and I am more than capable of managing whatever the Army throws at me – just not the sun. But I am not actually resilient. I am determined to pass because it means I can keep moving, never pausing to consider the events of my life, specifically of my childhood, that have pushed me to this point and to this place. At heart, I am a scared little boy, angry and confused, and have neither the capacity nor the inclination to ask myself, 'Am I resilient, or am I just running from childhood trauma?'

I run out of water. The checkpoints I pass have nothing left to drink by the time I get there. I have puri-tabs, which will make fresh water drinkable, if there is any, but instead of a creek there are just lines of dry rocks. I know I am in real trouble.

I don't remember much of the last hour or so. I recall at a checkpoint being told that I only had one more checkpoint to get to and I would be finished for the day. I remember the staff asking me if I wanted to quit. I said 'no'. If I quit, that would have meant failure, and this wasn't an option. I think I lost consciousness not long after that exchange. I came to and quickly passed out again. Drifting in and out of consciousness, I remember knowing that there was no way that I would quit, there was no way I wouldn't make the cut, there was no way I wouldn't be in the SAS. I would go until I died, and that's all I cared about. I am unstoppable, and I am unbeatable. My mind is fixed, and I will prove my worth.

It turns out I was beatable after all. I was stoppable, and it didn't prove my worth. I remember being unceremoniously hauled into a Land Rover. I remember having a thermometer inserted where I prefer nothing would go in, and I remember being told I hadn't passed the Special Forces selection. I remember being too dehydrated to cry. I didn't know it at the time, but I wasn't the only one struggling that day. The exercise I was on sadly hit the headlines when it led to the deaths of three soldiers in the extreme heat. People died that day and I survived, but all I could focus on was my own deep, dark despair. I started the day an unbeatable machine, the epitome of 'green, mean and keen' and ended it lying face down on the grass, with a sore bum hole, a head full of regret and a really bad headache.

This isn't a tale of resilience. It would be easy to frame this as a lesson to never give up, to give yourself the best chance of passing something if you refuse to quit, and I agree that is true. But it is also true that in order to be resilient, you must be focused on the *right* things, no matter what these might look like to you. I wasn't on SAS selection for some intrinsic reward, or a sense that I wanted to push my boundaries and discover the limit of my strength. I was on SAS selection because *I didn't like myself.* I didn't like the insecure, weak and angry little boy that I was, or that I perceived myself to be. I didn't stop when I should have because I didn't value myself enough to stop. Instead, what I did was prove my lack of emotional intelligence and my lack of maturity. I was there because I lacked mental resilience. I was still trying to escape what I actually was and to cover it up with a fake bravado – something I had done my whole life. The truth was that I was scared. At the core of my being, I was lonely and unhappy, and that does not make for a resilient mindset. I wasn't trying to be in the SAS, the most elite special forces unit in the world, for any altruistic, patriotic desire to serve my country. I was running away from who I was. And I'd been running for as long as I could remember. I was escaping facing myself, looking in a mirror and analysing my own ugly behaviours.

This is the core of what we're seeking to explore in this book. We're looking at the actual source and development of resilience, the authenticity and vulnerability that it requires, the devastatingly honest conversations and the personal growth needed. It took huge failures to find mine, but doesn't it always? Don't huge, ego-stripping moments reveal who we truly are? Doesn't a crushing defeat actually fill us with great clarity? How incredible would it be to be able to wilfully examine ourselves without the bias of our own ego? To be able to consciously strip away our pride and really see ourselves and our behaviours, to challenge and change perspectives and, ultimately, make decisions based on what we authentically want. 'Know thyself' has never had greater meaning than in the development of resilience. It is at rock bottom, when we are stripped of any ability to fight back, when we're exhausted, bested and beaten, that we truly reveal who we are. Once there, we can start to build.

An education

After I failed selection for the SAS, things took a real downward turn for me. My marriage broke down, I had a serious parachuting accident and my mental health fell apart. If it wasn't for my Army dad, Lee Soper, storming into my room (not deliberately or aggressively, he's just 6 ft 6 in and built like a vending machine) and demanding I help coach strength and conditioning at Colchester Rugby Football Club, I may not have been here at all. I would not be writing a book, I would not be helping lots of people through counselling and psychotherapy, I would not have the wonderful relationship with my daughter that I have now and I would not be feeling challenged and fulfilled in life.

I did originally think about declining his offer. I was overwhelmed enough as it was, miserable in a broken-down relationship, physically injured, struggling with parenthood, and battling my mental health. In that moment, I didn't actually want to be a strength and conditioning coach. But after a brief moment (and some strong words from Lee), I realised I really did want to be a strength and conditioning coach, mainly because at the time I was convinced my 'no' would have earned me a thump and/or scorn, or would just be ignored and I'd be dragged there by my hair. (None of this is true, Lee is a big softie really.) So I said yes, and soon after, I fell head over heels in love with coaching and mentoring. The initial 'no' was coming from a place of hurt, of insecurity, and it was Lee's strong encouragement that helped me to take those steps – for which I am eternally grateful to him.

I loved the positive effect I could have on the young players, some of whom went on to be very successful. After a year, this level of coaching and mentoring led me to apply for the role of Army

Parachute Jumping Instructor, the first of its kind, to help support the Royal Air Force (RAF) with the backlog of young paratroopers in desperate need of completing their basic parachuting course or re-training. I thoroughly enjoyed this job. While there I sent an email to the Army headquarters detailing how the mental health support for soldiers could be greatly improved. There was so much focus on rehabilitation following trauma or serious mental health issues, but barely anything on how to prevent these, or how to mentally prepare soldiers for dealing with traumatic events. There was hardly anything taught about developing the key psychological skills of resilience and managing emotional states, and, if there had been, the programme would have been so small that soldiers didn't even know it existed.

Soldiers like me who had struggled with their mental health had been floundering, not really receiving the direct support from an inadequate medical system (although it has since vastly improved). I felt convinced we should be teaching the principles of anxiety regulation and emotional intelligence, not waiting for soldiers like me to be in a catastrophic state – and believe me, there were individuals far worse off than I was, who struggled immensely and could only receive the help they needed once they had reached the self-diagnosed stage of 'fucked'.

The Army headquarters agreed with my analysis, and I was recruited from the parachute training school to their base, where I became the second in command of the British Army's mental resilience training team and was charged with the delivery of resilience training in the south of the country. The development and subsequent delivery of a mental resilience training package taught me huge amounts about the human psyche and its representative behaviours.

I saw and spoke to literally thousands of soldiers. I found that there were some incredible perspectives and ideas around resilience. Some of them educated me with their experiences and life stories, and showed attitudes and behaviours I had not yet began to consider. Others didn't believe in the training full stop, and I learned from them too. In their unwillingness to look introspectively and have the conversation with themselves about their behaviours, or to look objectively and question their emotional intelligence, they showed me that not everyone shared the same beliefs that I assumed the vast majority of the military had. This taught me huge amounts about the subjective lived experiences of people and the nuances of human behaviours. I think it is easy to see the military as one enormous, homogenous being, but it isn't. It is full of brilliant and inspiring individuals with their own subjective views and opinions, dreams, ambitions and lives.

*

While at the Army headquarters, I started my formal studies by diving into sports psychology. There are strong links between how an athlete and a soldier are required to respond physically and emotionally. They both need to manage fear and responses to orders and are under intense pressure to perform. They encounter complex tasks in a very small window of time, cope with external expectations and validations as well as wins and losses with huge consequences, and have to be adept at risk taking, decisiveness and leadership. I do miss those early days, hearing individual tales of strength and heroism in so many different forms.

I visited individuals who had served in Iraq and Afghanistan and along the way reunited with people I hadn't seen for years. I sought out medical teams that had conducted unbelievably complicated surgeries on wounded soldiers and civilians and heard their tales of heroism. I met great athletic champions who had broken world records and all previous expectations of what the human body and mind were capable of. I could see the connection between the two – the high-performing soldier and the high-performing athlete – in terms of mindset and cognitive capacities.

The British Army is full of some of the best that humanity has to offer the world. It was these powerful people who shone so much light on to the realities of the psychological models that I was studying. They taught me far more than any textbook ever had. I had been conditioned by my maroon-beret background to believe that resilience only existed in the form of mud, sweat and tears, carrying huge amounts of weight and screaming bloody murder with a weapon in your hands.

But resilience is not just restricted to the military, the blue light services or the extreme acts of endurance of athletes. Resilience is for *everyone*. As my studies went on, I saw traits of resilience almost everywhere I went: in the single mums who have to get up and show up every single day; in those with chronic illness; in those with long-standing, debilitating mental health issues who are in a constant battle with their own mind and mood; in office workers grinding out day after day to put food on the table for their families.

Resilience is the emotional robustness to succeed when there are many inevitable and obvious reasons to quit. Resilience is working towards any goal, whether you are in a suit or a green uniform. It is early mornings and late nights. It is surviving. It could be a hidden battle that nobody knows about. It is endurance and adversity. It is courage and beauty.

*

A few years into running the resilience training team, I stepped away from the British Army. After 14 years of service, I decided that I wanted to see what I could accomplish on my own. I became self-employed and slightly addicted to education. I became a qualified psychotherapist during the Covid-19 pandemic, the long periods trapped inside meaning that I finally found the time and focus I needed to pursue this ambition. Since then, I have worked with Paralympians, supported members of the Special Forces, and delivered courses to huge companies in London ranging from insurance and building companies to the Liberal Democrats in the Houses of Parliament, to Police Scotland, Thames Valley Police and Derbyshire Police, the Fire Service and the NHS. Some of them are so well known that I can see their billboards when travelling on the train into London, giving me a slightly self-indulgent feeling of pride.

I felt incredibly honoured to be asked to deliver a speech at Oxford University about effective communication with veterans in the mental health care system. After this incredible experience, I was invited for an interview for King's College and, unbelievably, I began my master's degree in war and psychiatry with a focus on the effects of war on mental health. I researched all sorts of theses. How does war change a person? Why does a person choose to go to war? What happened in their background for them to choose this potentially damaging path? What effects does it have on them, and how can we reduce these effects? What can we do, and how can we do it better for these people? I wanted to see how we could utilise our collective knowledge of human behaviour along with effective communication to help even the most traumatised, terrified, alienated and disillusioned ex-service personnel find their resilience again and live their lives with the fulfilment that they deserve.

The formal studies I have done so far have helped me enormously. I'm constantly challenging my own thought processes because I have to justify everything that I write in my academic work. I have to consider different perspectives every time, along with my own biases. I find this incredibly liberating, since it takes me away from my own beliefs and assumptions. And this, in turn, opens me up to new avenues of mental resilience.

*

I work as a psychotherapist now, utilising the therapeutic practices of CBT. Rather than focusing on a philosophy, such as Freudian or Jungian, I draw on the observable aspects of behaviour and their corresponding brain functions to highlight exactly what is happening to a person when they struggle with something, and why. I like the idea that the brain is plastic and malleable, and that in order for us to successfully manage our lives and develop resilience, we can unlearn negative behavioural patterns and replace them with positive ones. This even works when the behaviour stems from childhood trauma. After all, as Mohammed Ali said, 'It isn't the mountains ahead to climb that wear you out; it's the pebble in your shoe.'

I have all manners of cases and clients, from the anxiety-ridden chief executive officer who doubts their own decision-making process at every turn, to the athlete striving for that gold medal. The thing that unites all of them is the human spirit's intrinsic desire to find fulfilment, and the difficult journey that we must all endure to find it, which is where resilience comes to fruition. The seed of that fruition lies in education: to understand the role of the brain and the areas within it and the complex patterns of neurons and synaptic connections that formulate thoughts, ideas, behaviours and beliefs.

One of the tenets of my method is the understanding that whatever we have learned, inherited or been conditioned to believe can be unlearned, unconditioned, replaced and un-believed. Our lives and the way we live them are a direct reflection of what we believe to be true about ourselves. These beliefs are given to us by parents or carers, teachers, friends, enemies and our life experiences, ranging from the joyful to the traumatic, and they inform our self-worth and self-esteem.

It's crucial to understand that we cannot perform beyond our own level of self-worth and self-esteem. What I mean by this is that we cannot achieve beyond what we, at our core, believe we can achieve. This is where resilience comes into play. It is our ability to challenge and change these beliefs. It is the power we hold to reframe our beliefs about ourselves, our ability to change for the better while accepting the reality of our limitations. It is our capacity for real, meaningful development. It is our strength to grow. Resilience is ultimately the difference between seeing adversity in a situation, or seeing adventure.

In this book, I will teach you how to build mental resilience. I will do this by introducing you to a model called the Five Pillars of Mental Resilience, which is the idea that an individual's mental resilience is supported by five key building blocks: confidence, emotional intelligence, physical health, goals and relationships. Each pillar is represented by a chapter in this book. Each of those chapters contains a detailed plan on how to develop each pillar to maximise your mental resilience using the MIND method, which will be explained later. The foundation for your Five Pillars consists of genetics, taught behaviour and experience. We'll get onto that later too.

This book isn't filled with incredibly impressive feats of military achievements and operational service. I don't have those stories to share. It just wasn't what my service was like. I did serve in Afghanistan, I patrolled and lived in a military base and there was the inevitability of Afghanistan there, the tragedies and fear and moments of great humanity and camaraderie. I did my small part in Helmand. I wasn't an incredibly brave or even noteworthy soldier there. There were many who were – amazing and brilliant people – but that's their story to tell. I just have mine. Mine is about how my childhood and formative years shaped me into the person I am. It's about the disasters in my life (mainly of my own making), the sporting and world records I achieved, and the delivery of mental resilience training to the audiences, clients and people I have been honoured to train and support. This book teaches you what I have taught them and what I continue to teach today about mental resilience.

WHAT IS
MENTAL RESILIENCE?

I am on board a C130, a military aircraft used extensively for military operations, for both the transport of kit and personnel. It is designed with a door at the back, known as the 'ramp', and two side doors, which are used to parachute from. The Airborne Forces use these doors to mass insert troops to a designated area. Effectively, you are a human mule with a parachute, laden with kit, cramped into a green metal tube with a door either side. This particular squeezing of soldiers into a tin is for an exercise jump into Kenya and is designed to show the capability of the aircraft: how it can be used to despatch airborne soldiers, kit and equipment, how it can land in difficult terrain, and how versatile that makes it as an aircraft. However, predictably, things have already gone wrong. First, the aircraft hadn't landed on the dusty airstrip to pick us up until the midday sun was beating down, instead of early morning as it was supposed to. Soldiers were sitting for three hours with no shelter in the equatorial sun, in full parachute kit and equipment, sweating, sighing and hungry. If the purpose of military exercises is to highlight things that could be done better, there were plenty of lessons there.

The aircraft had eventually landed and we'd helped each other up, dutifully grabbing forearms and pulling each other to our feet, and we'd taken off with a distinct air of urgency. Now, we are finally on board the aircraft, and it is unbelievably hot and uncomfortable. Very soon after take-off, the distinct and triggering smell of sick invades my nose. Someone has thrown up and this quickly sets others off; before I know it, sick is trickling down both sides of the aircraft.

I don't want to be here. I look across to my signaller and I realise he doesn't want to be here either. All colour has left his face and he's wobbling. It is not fear but exhaustion that has drained him. His eyes roll back, and while perched on my ridiculously overweight kit, I witness him faint. At the exact same time, so do two other soldiers. In total, four people faint on the aircraft.

Regardless, with kit fully fitted and wobbly knees, we line up to jump out of the aircraft. The green light turns on and everyone shuffles towards the door, dragging their kit before turning 90 degrees and throwing their entire weight at the door. It's brutal, and those who volunteer for these exercises are some of the toughest and most determined people you could ever meet. But by this point, that level of motivation and resilience is wavering. My legs are shaking, and I realise that my static line (the line that pulls open your parachute and remains attached to the aircraft) is now my only balancing aid. I am gripping it with both hands, pulling some of my weight off my feet as I beg for that green light to come on.

Three steps before I reach the door, every single Airborne Forces nightmare happens all at once. I'm exhausted and disorientated, and I trip. Everything happens in slow motion. Gasping, I reach out as I lose my balance and let go of my static line. I reach out to the RAF dispatcher, desperately trying to gain control, but I miss and stumble sideways. I fall over and slip out of the door of the aircraft.

I remember the RAF dispatcher's face, frozen in shock, watching me fall from the aircraft, tumbling backwards into my own deploying parachute. What happens next starts a wave of panic. I spin out of control and shout as loudly as I can, 'Steer away, I am in twists!' It comes out as a series of shrieked expletives. Not ideal.

In all the chaos and lack of control, I can't find the handle to get rid of my kit, so that it can hang beneath me by a rope. This is how a paratrooper lands without breaking their legs, the kit hits the ground beneath them, moments before they do. Landing with your kit, including weapon, ammunition, specialist equipment and batteries, is a sure way of hurting yourself. In a split second, I reach for my reserve parachute, but I hesitate. In low-level parachuting, your main parachute doesn't 'cut away', which means you don't pull a cord and the canopy disappears away from you. You are too close to the ground, and by the time the malfunctioning parachute has been released and your reserve deployed, you would hit the ground. There is no time for that here, it takes too long. Instead, if there is a malfunction with your main, you must pull your reserve parachute, which is packed and attached to your chest, but pulling a reserve parachute means that it will erupt forward on a spring and then upwards as it inflates, and this will run the risk of collapsing your main parachute so you only do this if it's one hundred per cent necessary. At this point, I have something above my head at least, so I decide not to pull my reserve parachute. I look down to the ground that's coming at me at terminal velocity, and I think about my daughter, the lads, the banter and idiocy that has surrounded my life and think, It's been a laugh. *I believe this is 'it' for me, the big 'it' people close to death have to face, the proverbial kicking of the bucket, the military slang of 'endex', the tombstone that would read 'Here lies an idiot'.*

Often, when people go through traumatic near-death experiences, their brain tries to erase the memory. After falling out of an RAF aircraft from 1000 feet, with a small amount of twisted and tangled canopy above me, I was apparently unconscious for 14 minutes. My good friend and medic Tooke informs me I was 'a proper mess'. The doctor on the dropping zone who saw my impact from a distance thought that I was dead.

I must give thanks for the incredible healthcare that I received that day. I remember being put on a spinal board and feeling as if I had taken a legendary body-shot-upper-cut combo from Mike Tyson. I remember when I tried to open my eyes it felt as if someone had stabbed me in the head. I remember being loaded on board an aircraft and the same RAF instructor who dispatched me saying, 'You'll be okay, bud, don't worry'. I remember coming to in the hospital and I was tied down to my bed. In pure Jason Bourne style, I had to wriggle free of my restraints to release myself.

I had my brain scanned and was asked many questions I didn't remember the answers to. I was told I had what looked like a bleed on my brain and was not informed until the morning after that it was not in fact a bleed, but a cyst, and that instead I had suffered an extremely severe concussion. The next few weeks were truly awful. A severe concussion can cause inflammation and hormone dysregulation, and I basically went from believing I was going to be okay to a suicidal mess. It was an extremely challenging period, and as if things couldn't get any worse, it caused another relationship breakdown.

Less than a year after this incident, on my first jump of my parachute instructor's course, this entire story replayed through my head as I stood in the doorway of an aircraft, once again in full kit ready to parachute. I took a breath, and the familiar cold hand of fear gripped me. I knew this moment would come and I had wanted it. I wanted to jump again, because I decided I would not let my parachuting accident buckle me. I realised that I had the mental capability to embrace my fear, and I had a responsibility towards myself to do just that. I wouldn't bow out of parachuting due to a terrifying incident that I had successfully recovered from.

Sure, my recovery had taken a long time and a huge amount of pain and effort, but eventually I was cleared fit to jump. At this time, I had been advised that nobody would judge me if I called it a day there and never jumped again. But the ability to choose when we must fight on and when we must let go is an extremely personal and intrinsic decision. I decided to stand and fight, and I am glad I did. During that jump, I felt the most overwhelming fear I'd felt since my childhood. But as I did as a child suffering through torment and abuse, I chose to stand and fight. I chose to fight because I'd suffered through worse, and I knew I could handle this. I chose to fight because I craved a connection with my 'tribe', my 'pack', my friends in the Airborne Forces, and I knew they wanted me to fight for them.

Resilience takes many forms. It can look like someone somehow walking away from a parachuting accident and after recovery jumping out of an aircraft again. It can look like performing in front of huge roaring crowds to earn a belt, a medal or a world record. But resilience can also be found in our day-to-day lives. It's parents who work themselves to the bone to provide for their families, single fathers and single mothers trying to keep their life together as the cost-of-living crisis rages on. It's children battling through their own difficulties and demons, keeping their attendance record high at school and sitting exam after exam, constantly being questioned and evaluated. It's teachers and social workers giving their all to desperately keep our youth educated and supported. It's police services doing everything within their power to keep people safe; paramedics saving lives day in and day out, exhausted from their long shifts; fire services rushing to the worst imaginable car crashes, head-on collisions with children trapped in vehicles, trying to get them to safety. It's doctors and nurses providing the best care that they can in the face of ever more brutal cuts to their funding and support. Resilience is everywhere, and it is not lacking in the modern world, despite what right-wing pundits try to claim with their notion of a 'snowflake generation'. It's simply not true. Resilience changes and adapts as do the people who so inspiringly wield it.

What it means to be resilient

What is resilience, really? You can ask a thousand people and every answer would probably be slightly different, but they will all contain the same core principles, such as 'the ability to keep going', 'endurance' or 'not giving up'. This is a fair assessment, but I would challenge one small aspect of these definitions. Rather than the ability to *survive* great adversity, I would suggest that resilience is rooted much more strongly in the ability to *thrive*. This means having the ability to transform a dire situation into a great personal challenge and subsequently a success, and even finding enjoyment in the process.

In my experience, veterans unanimously describe their service abroad with an element of affection. Despite the inevitable trauma caused by operating in a war zone, which more often than not creates huge tensions in their lives afterwards, they describe positive feelings towards the organisation they served, the environments they found themselves in and the people they shared these experiences with. Blasting across the deserts of Iraq; stumbling through the booby-trapped streets of Afghanistan; squinting up into sideways rain; clambering up the side of some miserable mountain: they generally remember these times of great struggle with fondness, and this is the very basis of resilience. It is the embracing of a struggle, a challenge, a problem or a trauma and facing it head on, strong and committed, with a plan, with a resilient mindset and with support from those closest to you.

The origins and myths of mental resilience

Let's start by examining the very culture of resilience, and picking apart the idea of being tough, brutal, savage and stoic. This is not a new concept. Resilient men and women have stood out for thousands of years. Queen Boudica, riding against waves of Roman legions, still has her emblem etched onto our money. Winston Churchill sits proudly on our five-pound notes, his words of great stoic rhetoric still used in schools. We struggle to compare ourselves to these titans of history, and this is understandable. For most of us, it's difficult to imagine ourselves facing a legion of sanguinary Romans, slicing a man in half with a broadsword on a bloody battlefield while crying out for freedom. The comparison feels wholly unrelatable. But that's not the parallel I'm trying to draw here.

For the last hundred years or so, we've scorned our emotional responses – and in particular the male responses – of fear, grief or pain. This is utterly preposterous and completely unhealthy. Our emotional reactions are nothing more than an automatic response, programmed and generated by the human emotional centre in the limbic system. And we need them: they have developed for our survival.

If you stand on a piece of Lego, you shout and swear from the pain. If someone threatens you, you either become aggressive and ready to fight, you freeze up or you flee the scene. When given a lingering kiss from an attractive individual towards whom we feel sexual attraction, the hair on our neck stands to attention. These are nothing more than emotional and physiological responses to external stimuli. They are all natural bodily reactions engaging with a situation in a perfectly healthy and normal way.

The notion that one physiological response to a stimulus is perfectly acceptable, like shouting in pain after stubbing your toe, but another is not acceptable, such as anger and embarrassment at a belittling performance review by an individual woefully ill-equipped to critique you, is completely ridiculous. We're not 'allowed' to be visibly upset when experiencing rejection, we're 'supposed' to suppress tears when harshly spoken to by an authority figure, and we're 'expected' to take life's blows in our stride without dropping our composure.

There's a widely accepted perception that some of our automatic emotional responses represent weakness, and that they are ridiculous, hysterical and incorrect. But here's a telling fact. Men and women both cry. They cry over injustice and pain, grief and anger, loneliness and loss, identity and insults, rage and fear. Men cry over broken hearts, just as women do. We all feel pangs when we are excluded in social situations. We all get hurt when we feel rejected. We all grieve when loved ones die.

It is essential that we cry. It is essential that all the aforementioned emotions are expressed and vented. It is essential that they are exposed, engaged with and embraced. If we run away, repress these responses or judge them as inappropriate and weak, we cause far more damage to ourselves.

But how do we learn to normalise and embrace our emotions? How do we develop a healthy relationship with our automatic responses? It starts with educating ourselves, and then applying that education to our experiences.

The biology of mental resilience

It's important that we understand the biological processes behind emotional resilience. This empowers us to understand what happens to us when we respond to stimuli, and why. It explains why we want to quit when things get tough, why we want to give up when everything seems stacked against us, and what we can do to manage, challenge and change that response. Let's start by learning about the human brain.

In the 1950s, cognitive psychology was a relatively new discipline, known as the 'cognitive revolution'. It started to quickly grow in popularity, so much so that in the 1970s, the practice of cognitive science (which studies stimuli and our automatic thought processes and responses) had overtaken the traditional idea of behaviourism (which mostly attributes our behaviour to environmental events). Cognitive psychology is about how we think, behaviourism is about how we learn through interactions with our environment, and cognitive psychology was now accompanied by a bulk of new research. Researchers began to understand that during any experience there is a neurological process whereby an individual perceives that situation, processes it and then reacts. Something happens, and we think about it, and there is an internal dialogue that we can alter to change how we feel about it. This discovery didn't have much scientific traction at the time as it wasn't particularly well understood initially. But the scientists who researched this part of human cognition felt it accurately explained the neurological process of decision making. From the Second World War onwards, this process was also mirrored by the development of computers, which functioned in a very similar way: a stimulant, a process, an outcome.

For the purpose of this book, we will focus on two distinct parts of the human decision-making process. First, we'll look at the conscious process of the prefrontal cortex. Then we'll look at the subconscious limbic system.

The prefrontal cortex is one of my favourite parts of the brain. The reason I like it so much is because of its complex wiring and its incredible capability to grow, learn, compute and realign. The prefrontal cortex is where our conscious thoughts live. It is our logic and reason. It's where we develop perspective and understanding. This is where most of our decision making takes place when we are calm, controlled and in a state of homeostasis. Although this part of the brain deals with all of our conscious thoughts, it's actually a relatively new part of the brain at only around 500,000 years old – not very long at all in terms of human evolution.

The prefrontal cortex consists of millions of brain cells, mainly neurons. These cells play a very distinct and fascinating role within the brain to essentially pass on information. A neuron looks similar to the root of a plant: it has its main body, and it branches off into smaller parts. At the end of these branches are synapses. These synapses pass hormones, called neurotransmitters, from one neuron to the next, which instigates an electrical pulse up the main body of the neuron. So, a thought is really nothing more than an exchange of hormones and electrical pulses from neuron to neuron.

Sometimes these neurons will instigate movement through the stimulation of a motor neuron, whose role it is to allow communication between the brain and the spinal column and the muscles and organs of our bodies. So, when a motor neuron communicates with the central nervous system, this instigates a physical movement.

Within the prefrontal cortex, there are more synaptic connections than there are stars in the entirety of our milky way. In a way, you could say that you are capable of greater conscious thought than the entire breadth and depth of our galaxy. It is an incredible power to have, and later on in the book, when we discuss the key skills of resilience, we will examine how people strip themselves of this power by assigning the decision-making process to elements outside their control.

The second part of the brain we will explore is the amygdala, which is part of the limbic system. The amygdala manages our subconscious, emotional responses. It resides in the very centre of the brain and from the moment we exit the womb, it begins to learn and react to ensure survival. It is wired to want and need our survival, and a key part of this is gaining and maintaining tribal support. It drives us towards desires. It demands food and sleep and a safe position in a social hierarchy. It craves power, influence and strength. This part of the brain is what Freud called the id; it is a wild, anxious, envious and angry little caveman that lives in the centre of our brain.[1] The wonderful thing about this tantrum-throwing caveman is that it has kept us alive for millions of years. Its instinctive, egotistical and animalistic responses have helped us survive and thrive in a world that was once a very dangerous and unpredictable place.

Human evolution has taken millions of years. It's a strange concept to us now, but for nearly 99 per cent of our hominid history, killing for food was the only way for us to survive. Our bodies evolved to hunt and to kill, to fight for our territory, food and resources. We learned to dance around the fire and sing to form close bonds with our tribe to support us and keep us safe. And we learned to control what we can, and embrace what we couldn't explain as the will of the divine.

Our daily dramas would revolve around fleeing from predators, then gathering the rest of the hunters of our tribe, arming ourselves, ready to chase, catch and kill the predator that threatened our survival. It involved keeping our offspring safe from harm, hunting, killing and dragging back the biggest beasts in the field to roast over an open fire, providing sustenance for our brood. We endured millions of years of hardship and survival to evolve into the dominant species on our planet.

The amygdala has played a vital role in human evolution. It's because of this little part, nestled in the centre of our brain, that a caveman would immediately have a fear response when facing a hungry wolf. This fear response then triggers a physical response, the famous flight, fight or freeze response. If it wasn't for this part of our brain, we wouldn't have survived.

In the millions of years humans have existed, we've changed tremendously as a society. We didn't exactly go from cavemen to stockbrokers in a day. And we've now encountered a problem. Our culture and society have evolved much faster than our bodies have. Biologically, we are not built to cope with the excess of stimuli the modern world throws at us on any given day. Equally, we're no longer being chased by sabretooth tigers, hunting woolly mammoths or avoiding starvation and illness, having to face survival every day. In short, our bodies are designed for a world that no longer exists.

The stress response

Let's start with what we would consider our 'normal' state of being. The body is in a calm, controlled, content and comfortable state. This is known as homeostasis, where everything is at its resting rate and equilibrium. Our glucose levels are normal, we have mid-range blood pressure and pulse, non-dilated pupils, a core body temperature of around 37.5 °C, an even distribution of blood, calm digestion of foods in a comfortable sitting position, and good levels of hydration. The body is as content as can be.

The amygdala always craves this perfect state of homeostasis, as it means survival. It means safety and chemical balance, and there is stability for organs to function optimally. The amygdala wants safety in numbers, warmth, food and all the other necessities that ensure homeostasis can continue. The best thing about homeostasis is that it is self-regulatory. All we need for it to occur is comfort, being well fed and safety. There's no conscious effort required: it's our default setting, it's almost factory reset. A world in homeostasis would be a serene place indeed, but unfortunately something always disrupts the balance in the form of internal and external stimuli.

The prefrontal cortex, where our conscious decision making takes place, is constantly weighing up options and deciding what action to take based on the information that's provided. When a stressor appears, our homeostasis is disturbed. A stressor is anything that's disruptive to this state of perfect equilibrium. For example, you're driving your car and a reckless driver suddenly swerves in front of you. Without a moment's hesitation, you slam the brakes, and the car screeches to a halt.

So what has happened? Everything moved far too quickly for you to consciously process anything. People in these kinds of situations often describe not thinking at all, they just remember acting, with no conscious reckoning. This is because every single thing you see, hear, smell, touch, taste and experience is checked for danger by the amygdala. The moment the amygdala senses a threat, it turns to another part of the brain immediately adjacent to it called the hippocampus. The hippocampus manages our functions of feeling and reacting and gives a series of options linked to memory, in this case 'slam on the brakes!' This message is passed to the central nervous system, and the brakes are immediately slammed on. At the same time, there is a huge release of the stress hormone cortisol in the brain, aimed at the hypothalamus, which activates our flight/fight/freeze response and our physiological response to threat.

After this driver unceremoniously swerves in front of you, and once your car has come to a halt, you may curse, shout, honk or flash your lights, and you may even be tempted to speed ahead to return the favour. Clearly these are not rational things to do, and you are definitely consciously angry now. You no longer have just an unconscious physiological response to the stressor; you also have a conscious psychological response. You can hear the voice in your head, furious and irrational, goading you to a behaviour that could be potentially dangerous, each thought accompanied by waves of adrenaline and cortisol, now creating your own cycle of stress and anger.

The amygdala has a direct line to our prefrontal cortex, the part known as the ventro medial prefrontal cortex, linked to the amygdala and our emotional state and conscious cognitive reasoning, where there will be a conscious weighing up of risk versus reward. This is where we can reason with ourselves about what the most appropriate conscious response should be. Our psychological response, and the emotions that feed it, lead to spontaneous actions, such as the cursing, shouting and honking mentioned earlier. These are reactions you can't really fake as they're so instantaneous. And this is the part of the stress response process where a person's resilience can really shine.

What are emotions?

Think back to a time where you felt a physiological response to threat and danger. Suddenly time is moving slowly. Everything appears dreamlike, and your conscious thought cuts out. Your pupils widen, letting in as much light as possible, allowing you to perceive all threats. Your mouth goes dry – your body no longer wants you to salivate. A freezing cold feeling reaches your stomach, caused by capillaries shrinking away from your digestive system. Your body no longer wants to waste energy on digesting food, and all energy is now fed to the flight/fight/freeze response. A sudden gasp of air means your lungs are opening their airways, getting as much air in as possible. Your heart is pounding, and your blood pressure rockets, pumping blood to your muscles and anywhere else it needs to be so you can move suddenly and quickly out of harm's way. All of these physical processes happen in a split second. It's truly incredible how our body and mind co-ordinate these completely instinctive, built-in processes, priming us for survival.

These are all examples of our body's fear response, and fear is an example of an emotion. Emotions are deeply ingrained in our genetic code, and again the amygdala plays a vital part in why they are generated. According to psychologists Paul Ekman and Wallace Friesen, pioneers in the field of emotion research, there are six basic emotions that humans experience: happiness, sadness, fear, disgust, anger and surprise.[2] Emotions are irrational, non-thinking responses that have one goal: to ensure survival.

Without happiness, we wouldn't seek out human connections which are so vital for tribal survival. Without disgust we wouldn't be able to subconsciously assess whether a carcass is still edible, and we would risk eating something that could made us deadly ill. And, to give a more modern example, without surprise, we wouldn't slam on the brakes when a car swerves in front of us. Our subconscious, and the emotions that stem from it, are wired towards survival only, and all of our behaviours and needs serve that same goal.

The ability to understand and manage these emotions is the key to being mentally resilient. It is effectively the fundamental difference between a *feeling* and an *emotion*. An emotion is a physiological response – a sensation within your body and a change of the homeostasis within your brain – and is subconsciously driven. The conscious realisation and meaning that you apply to that emotion is a feeling. For instance, the knot in your stomach when you spot your ex at the gym for some might be felt as excitement, while others interpret that emotional response as fear.

Now imagine what it would be like to not get overwhelmed by your emotions. Imagine facing a daunting challenge and feeling fear, but not letting it affect your actions. Imagine facing a devastating loss, but instead of sadness taking the wheel, you remain in charge of your decisions. Imagine being able to calmly step away from someone who insults you, no matter how badly your anger wants you to take revenge. Imagine meeting any challenge life throws at you head on, remaining in control of your emotional state, calm, focused, stoic and resilient, while also being aware and embracing these emotions as natural reactions to stressful events.

Please note that at no point in this book will I ever tell you to suppress, ignore or dismiss your emotional state. In fact, I will actively encourage you to do the opposite. The more aware you are of your emotions and how they are affecting your decision-making process, the better you will be at managing them. It's impossible to control something that you refuse to acknowledge or accept is even there.

PREPARING THE GROUND

To help you develop your mental resilience, I have devised a model. It takes the shape of a series of pillars on a foundation. The purpose of this book is to teach you how to develop these pillars using the MIND mnemonic device (more on this later), and to give you the skills you need to build and maintain a resilient mindset. This way you can make real, lasting change to your life.

RESILIENT MINDSET

CONFIDENCE — EMOTIONAL INTELLIGENCE — PHYSICAL HEALTH — GOALS — RELATIONSHIPS

GENETICS   TAUGHT BEHAVIOUR   EXPERIENCE

Let's break down the main features of this diagram step by step.

The foundations of mental resilience

The foundations of mental resilience can be divided into a person's genetic disposition, taught behaviour and their subjective experiences. Every single person has different character traits as a result of these foundations, and because of this will not experience the world the same way others do. The differences in our foundations determine which of our pillars of resilience are most affected by a stressor, and this affects how we perceive an event and react to it. Therefore, the same experience can have a profoundly different effect on different individuals.

The Covid-19 pandemic lockdowns are a prime example of this. We were all deeply affected by the pandemic, and the societal trauma we experienced should not be underestimated. But the isolation did not affect all of us the same way. While some of us (with office jobs, mind you) hated working from home for months on end and felt profoundly isolated, others thrived while finally getting a break from a stressful work environment with constant social demands. It's a great example of how experiences affect us differently. What's traumatising for you might be a mere annoyance to someone else, and vice versa. This is why it's so important to listen and show empathy when someone explains their emotional response to you. They might be deeply wounded by something that would only cause you a minor scratch. Individual life experiences and what they teach us about the world make up a large part of our foundations, and it's important to accept other people's trauma, even if you can't directly relate to it.

Genetics refers to our inherited biological code. In simple terms, genetics determine whether your eyes are brown, green or blue, whether your hair is curly or straight, whether you're predisposed towards certain ailments, and so on. There's more research now than ever into whether we can be predisposed towards certain mental illnesses. Our brains are also affected by our genetics, and this determines our ability to take in new information, how much new information can be absorbed, how we store it and how we adapt to it. This directly relates to our desire to survive, something our brains are incredibly proficient at. They are designed to keep us safe, to survive. Our brains are certainly malleable, which I'll come on to later.

Taught behaviour refers to behaviour we observe and are directly taught in our formative years. Our brain starts developing as soon as we're born, and learns by observing the world around us and establishing patterns of behaviour based on what we observe. Our primary influence comes from our caregivers, and in our early years we learn by osmosis which is, simply put, a pattern of observation and imitation. An emotionally resilient caregiver will model these positive behaviours to a child, who will then mirror them. Equally, if an anxious caregiver models anxious behaviour to a child, the child will imitate this too. Patterns of behaviour can indeed be passed down through generations. Taught behaviour can also refer to things you've been shown and taught by caregivers, in school or via sport and hobbies.

Note that taught behaviour is not the same as a skill. A taught behaviour is something you have observed frequently and imitate without thinking, whereas a skill is something you develop through practice by working very consciously and specifically on improving it.

Experience can be summed up as the events that we witness and the things that happen to us. Experiences have a profound effect on how we view the world and ourselves. For instance, if you grew up with dogs as pets, your view of dogs is likely to be positive, and you see them as kind and lovely creatures that bring you joy. But if you were chased by an angry dog or even bitten by one, you might view dogs as terrifying and dangerous. Experience is the wild card of the foundations as we can only have limited control over what happens to us throughout our lives. Some of us will simply experience more trauma than others, and some of us might be lucky and only come across a few challenging experiences. Everyone's experience is unique, and, as mentioned earlier, it's important to show empathy and not impose your assessment of the world on someone else who might have a different experience. What's a happy, playful dog for you might be a terrifying creature for someone else.

The Five Pillars of Mental Resilience

The pillars are what hold up our mentally resilient mindset. If a pillar falls, then far more weight has to be carried by the other pillars to support the roof of mental resilience. If a pillar is crumbling, then we use our MIND toolbox, which consists of our predetermined, planned, day-to-day, memorable and accessible set of instructions and processes to re-engineer and rebuild them even stronger than before. There are five pillars for a resilient mindset: confidence, emotional intelligence, physical health, goals and relationships. The method to build each pillar will be covered later in the book.

Confidence

This pillar represents our self-belief and self-assurance. We gain this from the victories and successes in our lives as well as success-fully handling our failures and challenges. Success is subjective of course, and it starts with taking baby steps towards the goals you set for yourself. Reflecting on past success as well as past failure can help you develop a solid appreciation of your own capabilities and limits. It's important to celebrate your achievements, whether they are big or small. I've seen the great feeling of achievement and reward wash over young soldiers when they first receive their parachute wings. In that moment, they brim with confidence, as they should. The trick is to use those moments of success as fuel to support your onward journey (while still being able to fit your head through the door of course).

Emotional intelligence

This is the most important and influential pillar. There's a huge amount to say about this topic. Understanding and management of the self are essential for cultivating resilience, and these take a long time to develop.

This pillar defines how we understand and process the emotions, feelings and physical responses we have in difficult or stressful situations. These are the kinds of situations that test our resolve and where there is great pressure on us to perform. These moments reveal the inner core of the individual. Remember, you cannot fake spontaneous reactions, so how you react in these stressful situations says a lot about your inner emotional landscape.

Developing this pillar will help you understand why you react the way you do and how you can improve these reactions.

Looking inward is a common theme of this book, because I don't believe in relying on anything external to gather the motivation you need to improve yourself. This motivation must be intrinsic and self-generated to have a real and sustained effect. You are the source of this motivation, and you are the only person who can dig this up.

Developing emotional intelligence is a key part of this – it is learning to look inward, deal with your trauma, examine your reactions, ingrained beliefs and prevailing attitudes and address them head on. It's up to you how you do this. Some people use CBT or psychotherapy, some prefer podcasts on self-development or reading books like this one. It takes emotional intelligence to not let your amygdala overwhelm you, it takes emotional intelligence to not be tricked by past trauma into the same destructive behavioural patterns. These are hard skills to learn and the process can be painful, but it's an essential part of living a fulfilling life. You must learn to master yourself before you can ever truly learn to master anything else.

Physical health

This is your body's state of well-being. Good physical health has a tremendously positive effect on our mental resilience. Equally, a body that's not cared for correctly can affect us negatively. Bad nutrition and hydration affect our physical and mental health. It's where a lot of us fall short. Part of this is poor education, and part of this is personal responsibility. After all, you can't expect your body to perform like a Ferrari when you pour cooking oil into the fuel tank.

Training your body requires discipline, but being active and exercising has measurable neurological effects that we will explore in detail in the chapter on physical health. But remember, your body and how it feels is a reflection of what you choose to consistently put in it, and the activities you put it through. If you want to maximise your chances of reaching your physical and mental goals, it means maximising your physical well-being.

Goals

In order to lead a fulfilling life, we require purpose and direction, so therefore we need a goal or a series of goals, something to focus on, an outcome, an end state, a way of quantifying this purpose. We need a structure to direct our energy through so that it doesn't become dispersed and ineffective. We all need a purpose. Why am I getting up early every morning? Why am I working so hard at my job? Why am I studying until late every day? Why do I read, think and learn? Why am I falling into bed exhausted at night? Finding your purpose will help you believe that each step is an onward one, and that our efforts are not in vain. We need to be able to honestly say that our lives have purpose and that we contribute to something larger, whatever this may look like to you.

You might already have this purpose, but without setting measurable and achievable goals in order to move towards this purpose, you'll get stuck. I compare it to being lost at sea and spotting land far ahead. You might have the motivation to get to shore, but if you don't know how to swim, you'll drown. You can have all the inspiration and motivation in the world, but without setting goals you likely won't get anywhere. It's the difference between *why* you want to do something and *how* you'll actually do it.

There are big goals and small goals, and it's important you work on both. Sometimes a big goal, like getting that dream job or running a marathon, can feel out of reach. It's on those days that working towards smaller goals, such as writing a great curriculum vitae (CV) or going for a quick run, can help us keep up our confidence while we take baby steps towards the bigger goals that give our lives meaning. Both big and small goals will help to keep us mentally resilient.

I've worked with people whose pillars had crumbled away except for their central goal. Despite hanging on by a thread, having that goal helped keep their focus until eventually they could rebuild their other pillars. We need goals and we need purpose, or else the roof of mental resilience soon collapses. Luckily, we can teach ourselves to habitually set goals and to make them a part of our identity.

Relationships

This pillar is a bit more volatile, and one that can crumble in an instant, bringing the whole structure down. You share your life with the people you keep around you, and this includes your victories and losses, so choose them wisely.

No man is an island, and we all crave a level of intimacy with others. Adlerian theory says that all problems we face are actually interpersonal relationship problems.[1] So, in this school of thought, if an individual was the single surviving entity in an empty universe, then they would actually be rather happy! But, of course, this theory doesn't hold up in the real world. We need social interaction of some kind. It makes sense from an evolutionary standpoint: our survival as a species has always come from our collective strength, from the tribe. We wouldn't have lasted as long, or have become so dominant, if every second individual was introverted and longing to be a hermit.

The relationships we have as a child become the bar by which we measure everything else later on in life. Keep those who encourage you and celebrate your wins, but also who show real honesty and are brave enough to critique you to your face, for these are true friends. By having positive and supportive people around you, you too remain more resilient.

We are all stronger together.

The pillars in my model for mental resilience hold up the roof, but they are only as strong as their foundations. If you understand and solidify your foundations through repetition and conscious effort, you can build (and if they fall down, rebuild) your pillars, shaping them with the lessons you learn in life. This is the way to build mental resilience, and if you can hold your pillar straight and upright, your contentment is within reach.

The MIND method

To help us build our pillars, I have developed a mnemonic device (how very British Army of me!), specifically designed to be applied to each pillar. I call it the MIND method, and it stands for:

Measurable success
Intrinsic motivation
Now, in the present
Dream big

Here's what this means in the context of mental resilience.

Measurable success

This is your goal setting. This is your ability to sit down and identify what you want to achieve, and, very importantly, how you'll achieve it and how you'll measure your success. Goal setting is a very powerful motivational tool, and I'd suggest that everyone sets goals for themselves throughout life. More often than not, our goals are vague and nebulous – they are rarely concrete, well formed and measurable. It's therefore extremely important that when we set any goal, we identify, in real terms and measurable steps, what we are doing to achieve it.

Perhaps even more importantly, we need to examine our behaviours and see if they're conducive to the goal we're trying to achieve. This way we can easily see whether we're really trying our best or whether we're simply paying a token effort towards it. Contrary to what you might think, I'm not a huge fan of an intricate plan using many small, rigid goals to achieve a better one. We all know the real world is not that simple, and that things change and shift all the time. We need to be flexible with our goals, otherwise we will lose motivation, which is why our attitude towards them is so important. Instead of a very detailed plan, we need to become the embodiment of the end goal and shift the steps towards it accordingly. Say you want a big promotion at work. You might be able to sketch out a plan of steps to get there, but external factors will always contribute to how this plan will work out in reality. Instead, you need to fully identify yourself with and embody the goal of getting that job. Getting the qualifications you need, dressing for the part and acting (at least towards yourself) like you already have the job will help you find the confidence you need to achieve your goal and maintain your motivation. In my experience of working with clients, people who identify themselves as 'athletes', 'gym rats' or 'fitness freaks' are those who absorb the lifestyle, and they are far more likely to achieve their fitness goals than people who say 'I'm going to start working out'.

Intrinsic motivation

This is the motivation that comes from within. There are two types of motivation: intrinsic and extrinsic. Extrinsic motivation comes from the outside and is arguably more 'military'. It's doing something because you have been told to do it by someone who has rank or authority. Haircuts and shaving are examples from my time in service. In the army, hair must be kept short and neat, and sideburns must stay level with the middle of the ear. Some sergeant majors take great pride in their ability to spot a lengthy sideburn at a hundred paces. The evidence that keeping your hair this neat is entirely extrinsic could be seen the moment we were deployed anywhere. Most obviously in Afghanistan, hair was unkempt, beards were bustling, and my special favourite, the moustache, was grown to extreme lengths. The moment that the external motivation was removed, nobody cared about being well-kempt.

Extrinsic motivation becomes an issue when it impacts our performance and we rely on it solely to get things done. For example, a lot of kids are dragged out of bed every morning by their parents, who demand they go to school, go to work or play a sport. When these kids leave the nest, the external motivator falls away, and they quite possibly evolve into young adults who sleep in until noon, leave their studying to the last minute and have stopped exercising, which affects their lives a lot more than an unkempt army beard.

In very small doses, extrinsic motivation works to get things done quickly, but it's not effective over longer periods of time. We start disregarding someone else's will for ours the moment they stop imposing it. This is why we need motivation that lasts, and intrinsically sourced motivation is far more powerful to drive yourself forward.

Now, in the present

This is one of my favourite topics, as I often have to explain to people that we are all biologically hardwired to be extremely anxious in order to survive at all costs and to panic about the slightest thing that might challenge that. It's this survival instinct that causes one of the greatest modern challenges for our species: to stay present.

Part of our survival instinct is to learn from past threats and from that predict future threats. This means we rarely observe the very moment in time we're actually existing when neither of these threats actually exist. This is the basis of mindfulness, which has gained huge popularity over the last few years and with good reason. The only moment we have is right now, and when we effectively live in the present, the past and future won't bother us.

Living in the present is an important part of developing mental resilience. Sensible planning is, of course, acceptable, but there is no point to preparing and planning for a hundred possible negative outcomes. Instead, try to focus on what the most likely outcome is and assess the situation when it occurs.

Dream big

This is your positive outlook on the future. It's your self-regulation through mental imagery and the mental rehearsal of success. You don't dream with an absent mind, you dream with the full engagement of all your senses, and this immersive dream building will convince your brain that your goals are within your reach. This involves framing tough times with a resilient but positive outlook and focusing on learning from failure and adversity, keeping a clear vision for success and a persistent will to push onwards. In order to dream big, you need genuine and deeply held self-belief so you can stay on the course you have chosen to sail and add ballast to that belief so that you can't be capsized by the criticisms of others. By dreaming big, you will start to know your worth and what you can do to maximise your potential here and now. Big dreams provide a map for finding the path that will fulfil you.

The MIND method can be used to develop each of the pillars, and in the coming chapters we will be exploring how to use it effectively.

CHAPTER ONE

Confidence

What you can expect to learn in this chapter:

- What we mean by 'confidence'.
- How we can generate confidence.
- How insecurity can strip of us of our confidence.
- How anxiety and confidence are linked.

I am waiting for the host to let me in on a Zoom meeting to discuss the possibility of starting my master's degree at King's College with the course tutor, Professor Edgar Jones. I can feel the sweat on my back, and I check my shirt again, well aware that when I sweat, I smell. Thank God he can't smell me through a computer screen, not that it stops me from sweating and worrying even more. 'The only way you are going to a university is to clean their toilets.' These words are ringing in my ears, since they were lashed at me from childhood. For the record, custodial work is a very respectable profession, and I would never dare judge anyone for the job they do to feed their family and live their life, nor would I ever weaponise someone else's lot in life as an insult. It's the intended implication of these words, from people who were supposed to care for me, that cut me deeply. I feel that I do NOT belong here, I feel that I am not that smart, and this is not some fake humility, this is the God's honest truth. I truly believe I simply am NOT that clever at all. If this was a run with weighted kit over difficult terrain for 15 miles, I would be fine. I would even be excited. But this encounter terrifies me, and I'm having to use all my psychological coping mechanisms to remain confident and stoic. My thoughts are racing: I am not armed for this encounter, I have no experience in this field, why would they even consider me for a place on this course? I have mental images of being let in, only to be faced with a hyena-esque laughing group of my mates, having pulled the ultimate prank on me. I sweat some more.

In the end, what actually happened was a lovely conversation between me and one of the kindest and warmest people I have met, who was far more interested in hearing about my military experience than he was in interrogating my academic ability or qualifications.

It was, in fact, the safety in the knowledge that I knew I could hold a conversation that gave me confidence during this interview. Much like a bird that sits on a branch, calm and not worried that the branch may break at any moment, because it knows it can fly. I thought, *I can handle a conversation and whatever he throws at me, it can't be worse than a chewing out from a superior in the forces.* Despite my initial worry, I managed to secure a place at King's College London to study for a master's in psychiatry and war. And therein lies a point about confidence: it is self-generated. It is a belief in oneself, and most people's self-belief is undermined entirely by a series of false accusations that they tell themselves, known as insecurities.

Confidence and privilege

Let's take a moment here to talk about privilege. It is a term that's coming up more and more, as it should, because it's very important.

The world that you are born into is not the same as someone else's. Because of certain characteristics that you are either born with or have inherited, life will come with a different set of challenges for each of us. Gender identity, race, sexual orientation, class and economic status are all things that affect what kind of experiences we have in life, and in turn these influence not only the opportunities available to us as marginalised groups, but also how we are treated and how we feel about ourselves. It would be extremely naive to say that all of us have the exact same shot at our goals in life. So, I need to make this clear here: building confidence is not a level playing field.

I can't personally speak to experiences that women, people of colour or lesbian, gay, bisexual, transgender, queer, asexual and intersex (LGBTQAI+) people have. I do not know what it is like to be discriminated against or structurally disadvantaged for these characteristics. But I can certainly tell you how being working class and coming from a low economic status has affected my life.

I grew up in poverty. I lived on a council estate in Witney, we did not have central heating, we collected stamps to afford our TV licence and electricity, and I nearly always wore charity-shop clothes. I know this is a fashionable thing to do now, but for me, if I was caught wearing those clothes as a kid by my better-off classmates, it was a ticket to being ridiculed.

I don't want to say that being poor as a child left a bitter taste in my mouth. Not at all. In fact, I really enjoyed some of the adventures I had on the council estate. Disappearing off with reprobates to find porn mags that had been thrown into the bushes. Stealing cigarettes and sweets from the local shop. Having fights with random kids only to be best mates again after all the punches had landed. But the idea that there was more, that I could even have what I have now, was never really something that I had considered. How could I? The motivation to do more, to try and become more, to push myself, relied heavily on my belief that I could be those things. A child abused and feeling abandoned by their father is only ever going to blame themselves. When a caregiver stops loving the child, the child doesn't stop loving the caregiver, they usually stop loving themselves.

There are so many people born with very little. In the UK, the cost-of-living crisis is creating an ever-increasing gap between rich and poor, between living comfortably and struggling for food and heating. At time of writing, according to Citizen's Advice, in the UK there are three million families facing crisis over the cost of food, with 37 per cent of people worried about how they will pay their bills in the winter.[1]

A little side note here: some of the people I grew up with would actually find the idea of this cost-of-living crisis mildly insulting – there has been a cost-of-living crisis for many, many years already. These people have lived in poverty for most of their lives. It's just that now, nearly everyone else is affected too, and it becomes more of a talking point.

I have a huge issue with people and media branding those who live in poverty as 'lazy' or somehow inherently bad for needing to rely on state support or turning to crime to pay the bills. I don't think people who say this quite understand what it's like to live in that situation, and the lengths you will go to in order to survive.

Living in poverty puts you at far greater risk of suffering abuse, being a victim of crime, having chronic illness, getting a poor education and having poor mental health, among many other things.[2] These are people, unlike me, who never escaped the abuse, the drugs and addiction, living hand to mouth (if that) while trying to support a family. The stress is immense. Ask yourself whether, if you had grown up in that kind of environment, you wouldn't turn out just the same.

Keeping all of that in mind, it would be extremely dismissive to say that confidence, which is moulded so much by the environment in which you grow up, is not detrimentally affected by being poor. And when that poverty intersects with other characteristics, that puts you in a marginalised group. According to recent research by the Labour party, 53 per cent of Black children, 55 per cent of Pakistani children, 32 per cent of children of mixed heritage and

27 per cent of Indian children in the UK live in poverty. This is compared to 26 per cent of white children living below the poverty line.[3] All devastating figures, but it's worth noting here that if you are white, you are less likely to be poor.

Coming from a low socio-economic demographic puts you at a far higher likelihood of scoring highly on the ACE test. ACE stands for adverse childhood experiences, and the test is a series of ten questions that will highlight how much of an exposure you had to traumatic experiences as a child. This then becomes a predictor of your lifestyle as an adult. If you score high on the ACE test, it means you are far more likely to be addicted to drugs or alcohol, suffer from poor mental health and live in poverty. This ACE test is pretty much the only test that most of my beloved ex-soldier friends will score 100 per cent on, which means that by and large, they had really traumatic childhoods.

To illustrate the daily mechanics of this, I'll give you one example from my friendship circle. Some of my friends have genuinely celebrated being able to drive the van at work. This may sound bizarre to some of you, but many of my mates learned to drive in their early twenties, not in their teens. This is because most of the money they earned at that age was needed to keep their household and family afloat. Every spare penny was then saved for the lessons, insurance and the car itself – assuming that nothing else got in the way, like needing tools, clothes, Christmas or birthdays, or someone falling sick in the house. So you can imagine, that saving up to get your driver's licence takes a long time in this situation, and therefore deserves a big celebration when achieved. To then be able to use this skill at work is a big deal, and I hope you see now why that is the case.

What about the people at the top of the food chain, who point fingers and say things like, 'Pull yourself up by your bootstraps!' or, 'It just takes hard work'? I'd argue that even though university policy might be all inclusive, the £9000 per year tuition fee says otherwise. I'd argue that my mate, who learned to drive in his twenties because it took him that long to save up, would struggle with coming up with this figure. And I'd also say that for many people in poverty, the idea of being saddled with massive student loans on top of their other financial burdens isn't exactly an attractive proposition.

Privilege is not about what you had growing up, it is about what you didn't have to do to get it. And this really affects your confidence. If you haven't had to struggle for the basic things in your life, then you will not see pursuing the building blocks of a successful life as a struggle. If doors are opened for you left and right, you will start assuming that doors are generally open for you to walk through. If you haven't heard 'no', then why would you ever expect to hear it now? Alternatively, if you hear 'no' all the time, and those doors are not only closed, they are locked, you'll have to put that much more effort into prying them open.

Class divide in the UK is genuinely terrible. It is your identity. It is how you are seen, and others believe they can treat you a certain way because of it. I have felt rejection because of my class. I have had my work corrected by someone else, even though I never asked for this feedback, perhaps because they felt I needed to be taught, that they knew better than the working-class chap who typed up the report. It's this genuine, unconscious idea that they were 'helping me' (as if I needed it) that they would not bestow on someone from their own background. Hilariously, their corrections were all wrong.

I have been ignored or not even considered for promotions and job opportunities, or discredited because there was another candidate with a more 'desirable' class background than me. These are such ingrained beliefs and systems that it's not even a conscious effort to push you out, it's part of the fabric of our society. It's literally everywhere, and it shatters people's confidence.

Here's another great example to illustrate this. It's well known that women are far less likely than their male counterparts to apply for more senior jobs or ask for a promotion or a pay rise because they tend to feel that they're not qualified enough, even if they are.[4] One brilliant female friend of mine has a way to get around this feeling of inadequacy: she asks herself, 'What would a man called Rupert do now?' Rupert to her is a white, straight, upper-class man with financial privilege and power. Rupert, in her mind, would brazenly send that email without second guessing himself. Rupert would apply for that job even though he only meets half the requirements – and he'd get an interview too! Rupert would do all these things with unflinching self-belief because Rupert has rarely been told no, and the doors were open for him to step through. I'm aware this is quite simplistic, and I don't want to imply that no one has absolutely no challenges in life no matter what their background is, or that all men called Rupert have it easy. It just serves to illustrate that a lot of us are aware that it's easier to have this level of confidence for some than for others.

For those of you who don't believe in the patriarchy and say things like 'but men don't have it easy!', let me tell you this. That is just the other side of the same coin. As a man, you do not get access to some kind of closed group with a secret handshake, which is why you might feel like this is all nonsense. But the point is that men and women *both* suffer under patriarchy. The expectation on men from this system not to show emotion (because that is 'weakness' of course), just to take it all on the chin and carry on without breaking, is one big cause of mental health issues among men. Men and women are both at the mercy of capitalism and our broken society and the systems within it. But because of how these systems operate, it just is statistically more likely that as a white, straight, rich man you get to sit at the top of it all.

Finally, let's talk confirmation bias. There are people who have dropped out of school and have come from poverty who have been successful, and therefore argue that the system works. They will say that, as long as you are willing to work for it, anything can be yours.

That's really great for you if that's what happened to you. But you need to be aware that you are a statistical anomaly, and this is by no means the rule for others. Work rate is absolutely a factor for success but by no means the deciding one. It's just the one you have control over. Opportunity, infrastructure and support all play a huge role. Statistically speaking, escaping poverty is a huge ask for those who are full-time carers for their parents, who only have access to food banks and atrocious school dinners (that took the efforts of a brilliant footballer to rectify, thank you, Marcus Rashford), who are poorly educated, have chronic health issues and little to no employment opportunities aside from a zero-hours contract.

So let me repeat what I said at the start. Building confidence is not a level playing field for everyone. For some, it can be much harder depending on their experiences and circumstances.

We are all diamonds

As humans, we place great worth on things that have rarity. Take diamonds, for example. Diamonds are expensive because they are rare, beautiful and shiny. We can buy diamonds on various online markets to invest in their worth, and we trade them. We forge them into jewellery and keep the pieces as family heirlooms. We build impenetrable fortresses to protect them. We write great movies about stealing them. We wear them on red carpets. And when we want to show commitment to one other, we buy diamond rings for each other. When you die, you can even have your body crushed and heated to the point where the carbon atoms form into a near perfect structure, and then you can become an actual diamond. Most importantly, diamonds are indestructible, and all are unique, with their own specific flaws and inclusions.

There is an analogy here that I want to explore further. Through a greater acceptance of yourself, through shifting to a more powerful way of valuing your existence and experience, through improving the choices you take on life's path, you can reveal your own true diamond self.

How many people in the world are there who are doing what you are doing? How many are doing it in the same way, with the same perspective, background, and life experiences? There's only one James Elliott that I know who has a daughter quite like my troublemaker, who does mindset and resilience coaching, who has a head slightly too big for his body, and a comprehensive knowledge of the Star Wars movies.

That makes me unique, but does it make me rare? My choices and decisions are leading me down my own path, and no one is taking the same choices in the same manner. There is no one else out there who is walking the same path that I am taking through life, and so the only conclusion is that I am perhaps rarer than a diamond. There is only one of me, one person with the experiences, attributes and characteristics that I have built up. I am unique, rare and therefore precious to the world.

In the same way that there is just one of me, there is also just one of you. I walk my individual path, and you yours. Therefore, if I'm perfectly sure in saying that I'm a diamond, then I am very certain you are a diamond too. You can know this by looking inward, minding your breath and asking, who am I and what path am I walking? Turn far enough within, and you will reveal your unique and complete experience. You are a diamond, no matter what you choose to do, because you are the only you doing it.

Let's go deeper into this, because what I'm talking about is not that revolutionary in the world of psychology: it's a rehash of Adlerian psychology. Alfred Adler goes even further than my diamond analogy. He posed that happiness – that is, *true* happiness – is identifying what makes you subjectively feel fulfilled.[5] It might be playing rugby, running, being a doctor, selling cars, reviewing food, or any other of the infinite actions and activities available to us. The facet of your diamond's existence that gives you fulfilment is also the key source of happiness. Adler argues – and I would nod my head in agreement – that if you do what you do, but you do it for money, recognition, or even to prove yourself to be better than others, then you will not find your sense of true happiness.

Doing something that fulfils you directly links to your confidence. When you see someone do what they love doing, don't they look confident? This is honestly something I absolutely love, and I'm lucky enough to see it quite often. Seeing a person doing what they're passionate about reveals their authentic self, and this person brims with confidence, which spills out to the people around them. No matter what they do, whether it's dancing or painting, running or kicking a ball, mentoring or teaching, singing and strumming instruments, when you do something you love, for the sheer reason that you love it, your confidence will overflow and spill onto others.

Adler also says that happiness stems from using that which brings you the unique fulfilment to help the community around you. Helping your community is where your diamond finds its purpose, its meaning and its role. The community – or 'tribe' as I like to call it – needs you, and you need them. Be the diamond that uses their unique abilities to reflect more light into the lives of others. It doesn't matter if your actions help people to laugh, think, grow, learn or any other positive life action. Your life's meaning is found in the betterment of others' lives.

The inevitable reply that I get to this 'be a diamond for others' idea is a laundry list of what that person perceives to be their character faults and personality problems – that is, all the things they don't like about themselves. This list is then used to deny their status as a diamond, and to reason how they might not be enough to bring joy to others' lives.

Now, it's true that no one is perfect: we all have things we can improve. That's the nature of self-development – making better choices requires some poor choices initially. But a person describing their behaviour as 'it is what it is', or 'it's how I am, and I can't change that', simply isn't being honest. It's not our place or our job to change the internal reasonings of someone, nor is it within our power. Our work is to ensure they understand that change is possible, and fully available to them if they so choose it.

People only change when they themselves want to change, not because someone else wants them to. People need to closely inspect their own prism of self, to recognise and identify faults in their own diamond. Then, through sufficient heat and pressure, meaning conscious energy, they can remould and perfect their diamond structure towards whatever form they deem as close as possible to flawless. The only person who has the energy and is in the position to make those changes is that person.

Your confidence and mental resilience will increase the moment you are able to see yourself as a diamond, and you can bask in the warmth and light that this analogy brings. One of the most impactful pearls of wisdom I give to people is: there is no such thing as rejection, only redirection. You can best understand this from the diamond perspective. When people say 'no' to you, they aren't being critical of your inherent worth – life is simply encouraging you to go where you are meant to be. In a sense, the faster the rejection comes, the faster you are walking along the right path.

Like many things in psychology, it is not always this simple, of course, just to see yourself as a diamond. Hypercritical parents will make you believe that you must achieve perfection every time at whatever you attempt, which is of course impossible, and the more you're expected to attain perfection, the more you believe yourself incapable of any achievement at all. You start undermining yourself at every step, hindered by the belief that you are not enough – it's a truly awful place to be in. The foundations of the Confidence pillar can be very fragile indeed.

When it comes to tackling this self-sabotage, I find it to be very effective to ask clients about how they saw their caregivers handle pressure. I hear a lot of stories where mothers and fathers would become emotionally volatile at the first sign of stress. A father's road rage for example, which would be terrifying, or an overwhelmed and stressed-out mother, shouting at her kids after a minor spill. This creates huge insecurity in the child (and later, the adult).

When we're young, our brain develops by observing the world around us, and our hippocampus grows in a process called neurogenesis. The age-old 'do as I say, not as I do' instruction our caregivers would chime at us simply contradicts how the brain actually works. It looks for the example set and mimics that instead. Consider this – when do children ever do as they're told when they have seen an adult, particularly a caregiver, do the opposite?

When we get to adulthood, a lot of us suddenly have the realisation that we're turning into our parents. And this is exactly by design – you are supposed to, because your caregivers teach you how to survive in your formative years. But this of course means we're also adopting their negative behavioural patterns.

So what negative taught behaviours did you observe? What was passed on to you by your caregivers that you now identify within yourself? Do you tell yourself 'I can't/would never do that, it's too difficult/scary/unrealistic/[insert negative adjective]' because that's what you heard your parents say about themselves? That means you've absorbed this. A tough spot to be in.

Attachment theorist John Bowlby put it this way: 'What cannot be communicated to the mother cannot be communicated to the self.'[6] This means that, whatever a parent can't teach themselves they will not teach you. This translates to unmet needs in childhood, which in turn manifest in our behaviours as adults. Lack of confidence often comes from growing up in an environment where the caregivers do not believe in themselves either. You can see now that the foundations of lived experiences and taught behaviour heavily influence the stability of the Confidence pillar.

We are all unique, we are all diamonds, and treating yourself as such will have a positive effect on your confidence.

Failure, success and impostor syndrome

Confidence is undermined by insecurities. I hear about insecurities more and more in my clients and it seems that more people acknowledge them and identify them as such in themselves than before. This could be an aesthetic insecurity, a personality trait or a behaviour that makes them feel less than, fragile, ready to break.

But they only have this worry because they don't see the beauty of who and what they really are. They are a diamond, admittedly with some sharp and rough edges, but a rare and priceless diamond nonetheless. Crucially, they would be a far happier diamond if they were to use their undoubted individual talents to help improve the lives of their tribe members. After all, if you pool a group of diamonds together, they shine even brighter. No matter what you think of your thighs, your lisp, your height, your laugh, your irrational fear of water, heights or deadlines, your funny habits that make you feel that you're different from everyone, or whatever gremlin spikes your insecurities, you are rare and beautiful precisely because of these things, and your tribe will appreciate you exactly as you are, flaws included. Insecurity, fear of failure, lack of self-worth and jealousy of others – they all impact our confidence and can all stem from not seeing ourselves from this diamond perspective. The only challenge is finding your role within the tribe that can help others to shine as you are.

I want to make it clear that this diamond isn't a metaphor for 'just being good on the inside', that there's a diamond somewhere inside everyone which you somehow need to unearth from underneath all your 'unappealing' traits. No, you are the diamond in your *entirety*, your external presentation included. Don't dismiss any part of yourself, as your self-worth fills up every aspect of who you are. If you understand that you're priceless, then you're likely to treat yourself that way, which comes with more self-respect for your body, mind and aspirations.

If you then experience loss or rejection, you are more impervious to its negative effects. You can examine the nature of the loss and work out how to fix it for the next time you face a similar challenge, but you don't let the negativity affect your innate self-worth.

If you can understand that all of you is shining beauty, then you can understand that your inability to reach the finish line first, missing that shot or not getting that job is not because you lack worth. It's because you lacked preparation, training, or perhaps sufficient application of your skills.

I have coached enough high-performance people to say with confidence that effort is (almost) everything, or at least in the sense that it is the one thing within your control. Those with incredible talents often let themselves down, precisely because they are born with a genetic head start. They rely on that genetic advantage and begin to develop a negative mindset towards training and practising. Those who understand the necessity of hard work from the beginning are often actually the highest achievers, not the people with the most talent. I think this is because they see that they had their work cut out for them as they weren't quite as gifted as other people, and so they developed an appetite for hard work and self-development.

Later on, it is this work ethic that separates the good from the great. If, in the early stages of their career, they would have accepted a loss as a final critique of their self-worth, they would never have reached those heights later. They are fuelled to achieve their goals because their lives are aligned to what fulfils them most, to do what makes them and their tribe happy.

And it is this diamond-attitude fulfilment, where failure is seen as a lesson, not a punishment or indication of worth, that protects them when a loss comes knocking. I say 'when' here and not 'if", because as we have discussed, all endeavours you'll ever undertake will suffer some kind of failure on the road to success. Failure is not a catastrophe – it's a fuel, it's a motivation. The diamond view of ourselves ensures we see it that way. We can see the lesson that must be learned, confident that the value of our diamond remains unchanged.

It's at this stage that we've enacted the principle of 'redirection, not rejection' and we recalibrate to try again. And after all, you needn't be so disheartened about your defeats. Remember, you're a diamond – the world's hardest naturally occurring material.

Now try it for yourself. Think of your success, think of what you are proud of, and where you have failed, and what the lessons of both those events were. See yourself as that diamond, and shine brighter than ever before. The first step to building your Confidence pillar is to see your authentic, unique power and strength for all that they are. You, my friend, are a diamond.

It is of course at this point that I'm usually met with the inevitable question: 'What if I fail?' People who are racked with fear of failure and unable to see past that fear often never step outside their comfort zone. They underestimate their ability to cope with a situation. They worry that their peer group will notice this and will rip them apart for even trying to push out of the status quo.

An equally terrifying and sad aspect of human nature is that if someone is trying to grow and achieve, we will often try to take them down simply because their activity is a startling reminder of our own inactivity. We are so sacred of this judgement and ridicule that most of us won't even dare to push a personal boundary and start that business, build that house, pump that iron or any one of millions of different avenues for achievement. It's awful.

But do not completely despair, there is a way of reframing that confidence-destroying fear of rejection from your social peer group. You need to reframe how you perceive 'failure'. I have put 'failure' into quotations marks here simply because I don't like the word and its connotations. The rule we have attached to failure is that if you pursue a goal and are unsuccessful for whatever reason, you should feel negatively about yourself and your efforts and this will, of course, discourage you from trying again.

I have a wonderful story about a man who perceived himself as a diamond, and therefore never quit. For the purposes of this book and the lessons that we can gather from his tenacity, and because he became a member of the elite special forces and we must protect his identity, we shall call him Mark. Mark was not always renowned for being the brightest of the bunch, but he was undeniably one of the fittest endurance athletes I've ever encountered. I met Mark on Special Forces selection; it was his third attempt. In terms of sheer will-power, this is as impressive as it sounds. But I was even more impressed when I found out that he'd already done a very elite unit selection, the Pathfinder Platoon's selection, three times before his Special Forces selection efforts. I was even more impressed because I realised the two courses share a near-identical 'hills phase' of selection.

So, to ensure we are all on the same page, this was his sixth time on the infamous hills. He knew exactly where the checkpoints were dotted across the vast distances around the infamous Brecon Beacons trail and, despite the fact that he'd been here several times before, he was unphased, showed no signs of demotivation, and before you knew it he was off again, up the next mountain.

Speaking to Mark during our free evening hours, it was clear how he had become so motivated to keep pursuing Special Forces selection. He made it clear to me that he knew where his talents lay, and what his role for his tribe would be. 'I just want to be Special Forces,' he said to me. 'It's what I'm good at, and this'll take the Mrs and kids closer to their grandparents. Everyone's a winner.' He had identified his sense of fulfilment in being a Special Forces soldier and had seen how his success could benefit his tribe.

He lost no self-esteem in the previous unsuccessful attempts, each time identifying where he went wrong, and he had improved those aspects of himself only to come back better, stronger and more skilled than before. He never lost faith in himself as a diamond, and he didn't take his multiple failures personally at all. Each time he could attribute his failure to factors that at that time were either out of his control, or within his control so he could work on them. But with persistence, training and self-application he would eventually influence those factors in his favour. That time, at his sixth attempt, he passed selection. The last time I saw him was on a counter terrorism training exercise, where he set one of the attack dogs on me. I think we are still friends.

Mark's confidence was through the roof as he simply understood that his chances of success – if we measure success as a subjective sense of fulfilment – relied on changing how he saw failure.

I am not naive enough to say 'if you enjoy the process then failure will never feel like rejection' or that 'if you enjoy what you do then you'll never find it exhausting'. I love writing, learning and studying, yet mistakes and 'failures' upset me. Case in point, in a previous chapter draft of this book, I mislabelled a certain theory within psychology and my editor picked me up on this. That felt bad, because this is my actual field of work – human behaviour and the theories that assess it – so I had to fetch an iced caramel latte and take a super middle-classed stroll through the park to forgive myself.

But my confidence didn't slip. I didn't think of myself as a failure. I didn't feel that I had embarrassed myself somehow. Instead, I thought to myself, *I'm learning. With every mistake, I will learn more, and I will improve myself.*

This is not to say I don't suffer from the classic 'imposter syndrome'. A lot of us do, and if you read this thinking you are the only one around you who does, I can confidently tell you this is completely untrue – we just don't talk about it to each other enough.

Someone can have all the skills, qualifications and experience in the world, yet can still feel completely unworthy of being in a job, their position in a sports team, on a university course, and so on. Not only that, they are worried that at any given moment, the mask will slip and the people around them will discover they don't actually belong there.

Because of this, we sit silently in work meetings, despite all our skills and qualifications, in an almost perpetual state of worry, terrified to speak up and voice our (often brilliant) ideas, because it might just be the exact moment when we will be discovered as a fraud, who just ended up here through dumb luck. We will be shamed back into the hole where we belong.

Sound familiar? That's because you're not alone. According to a recent survey by YouGov, more than half of Britons identify with at least four common signs of impostor syndrome, including difficulty accepting praise and compliments, having high expectations of themselves, more criticism of self than of others and downplaying their achievements.[7]

This is often quite simply because many people grow up never learning how to validate themselves. We don't know how to tell ourselves that we are worthy, and we don't learn to celebrate our successes and achievements. We were often undermined, invalidated and made to feel inadequate by caregivers, peers, or the circumstances and experiences in our lives that we have no control over.

Once I figure out how to completely eliminate impostor syndrome from my life, I will let you know. I'm not quite there yet. But one thing I've learned is that it is so common that it's likely that the people you look up to, whether this is at work, in your personal life, or your heroes in sports, music, film, literature and so on, have all felt like this at some point in their lives. It's almost an inevitable part of being human, and effectively dealing with it will fortify your mental resilience. There are a few exercises at the end of this chapter that will help you with this.

How confidence and anxiety are linked

I know that this may sound incredibly insensitive, but I find the neurobiology of anxiety very fascinating. I know that there are people completely debilitated by the psychological effects of this horrid feeling, and I feel very sorry for how disruptive it is to their lives. There are people who suffer so immensely that the smallest challenges can feel like huge problems, even if they are objectively manageable. It's a horrible state to be in.

It's important that we look at the causes of anxiety, both the biology and the psychology.

I have always liked the idea that thoughts and behaviours are a result of a measurable process, a quantifiable exchange of information and energy. I'm not the spiritual type – that butters no parsnips for me – so when I say energy, I mean literal pulses of electricity that stimulate cells, and therefore departments of the brain, into action. And, if there is something going in our brains on that we can quantify, observe and measure, then this can be changed and manipulated.

The biology of anxiety is a lot like the stress response described in the Mental Resilience chapter and will be covered in more detail in the Emotional Intelligence chapter. There is a perception of a threat, which causes a release of cortisol which ignites our sympathetic nervous system into action. There are cortisol receptors in most cells of the human body, and this stress hormone spurs certain parts of our bodies into action and deprioritises others that are not deemed necessary in that moment. Effectively, this is the brain's way of prioritising certain functions of the body over others to ensure survival.

Do you get butterflies at the mere suggestion of a meeting with your boss at work? Those butterflies are the reduction of blood flow to the digestive system. A fluttering heart when your ex's name unexpectedly appears on your phone? Your heart is pumping harder to get oxygenated blood where it needs to be to run away. Are you finding yourself coming up with increasingly irrational solutions in a crisis situation? Your prefrontal cortex is being heavily subdued and influenced by your subconscious, because it wants you to prioritise your physical safety.

This physical response can culminate in something that unfortunately is quite familiar to a lot of us: a panic attack. A panic attack is really an overwhelming sympathetic nervous system response. Maybe you've had one yourself, or perhaps you've seen someone else suffer one. In the latter circumstances, you've possibly seen someone simply sitting in a chair, hyperventilating, shaking and consumed by fear. As a bystander, often the thing that they're panicking about feels much less severe than the panic reaction of the person. In fact, sometimes the thing they fear objectively does not exist, or there is no causality between the event that triggered the panic attack and the outcome the person fears.

That doesn't mean, however, that they aren't real and shouldn't be taken seriously. I used to have them as a young boy. My mum has told me that I used to overpower her in my panic, desperate to get out of the house and run away from a perceived threat. I remember waking in the middle of the night and feeling as if everything was closing in on me. The walls, the bed sheets, my clothes all felt too close to me, and I needed to get outside. There was a latch I couldn't reach in the day, but during those nights, with my mind filled entirely with horrors, I could not only reach it, I even had the strength to pull the bolt back. I would shiver, sob and become irrational and uncommunicative. I couldn't understand how anyone wasn't feeling what I was. It was extremely isolating. I felt these huge waves of adrenaline, that seemed external to me, as if a huge power was trying to overwhelm me. After that moment, they would pass. I remember saying, 'Did I manage that one?' and my mum looking at me blankly. I couldn't work out why she didn't notice what I had noticed, and I wondered what was wrong with me.

I have had them as an adult too. I remember once sitting on the bathroom floor in my then girlfriend's home, covered in sweat, shivering and feeling those rushes of energy. I don't remember what triggered it, but I felt as if I wanted to flee, scream and cry. After some time I regained control of myself using breathing techniques, calming down my parasympathetic nervous system, and got back into bed. The next day my then girlfriend said, 'I didn't know what to do, so I thought I'd leave you to it.'

Anxiety can be extremely isolating when we don't understand that it is simply a hormonal response to a perception of a threat. And when the people around us have no idea what is happening either, this feeling of isolation becomes even more severe. For both parties, it is an overwhelming and terrifying experience. Therefore, I don't really blame my ex for her response – many people are simply ill-equipped to deal with others when they get into a panicked state like this.

Now, some people hold that whatever triggers you is what controls you. I find this a rather harsh statement. Some of our physiological responses to threat, which manifest as anxiety, aren't so much controlling us, but rather they are unprocessed traumas that instigate a disproportionate response.

There is a huge amount to be said for the effectiveness of sitting in therapy and processing what has happened to you in your past.

Engaging with a trusted professional in a safe environment to talk about the situations that bring you anxiety will help you understand why this happens, and single out the memories of events that trigger this response. Something may have happened a very long time ago, in a totally different context, and even if this has now passed and you regained autonomy, you could still be having this response and that's okay. Therapy will help you understand that your response needn't be one of fear and that you can reason through this fear. Along with some simple soothing techniques for managing the biological responses (some are found at the end of each chapter in this book), you can learn that your fears are irrational.

Of course, those fears don't feel irrational in that moment of panic, and sometimes the response isn't irrational at all. We had a discussion once at my university course about panic, and whether it actually even exists. A photo was shown of New Yorkers during the terrorist attacks on 9/11, fleeing the huge dust cloud from the collapse of the second tower on that terrible day. The newspaper that had printed the picture mentioned 'mass panic'. But was this really the case? If you were there, and you saw that tower collapse would you not desperately run away from that engulfing dust? Of course you would. This is not an irrational response, in fact the only person in that moment who was behaving in an objectively irrational way was the person who paused to take that photograph. So, if we define panic as an irrational response (which some people do), arguably this very logical response to a real threat does not qualify. Interesting stuff.

The key to figuring this out is the ability to distinguish a real threat from a perceived threat, and subsequently objectively assess whether you have the capability to deal with it. When you're anxious, you're led to believe by your body that your response is completely justified. And why wouldn't it trick you into thinking this? Based on your emotionally driven perspective, you should be terrified of the situation you're facing. That meeting with your boss is scary because your boss could fire you on the spot. You're sick at the thought of speaking in front of that group – what if they laugh at you? In that moment, you believe you wouldn't have the skillset required to deal with these situations, so your parasympathetic nervous system is doing the job it was designed to do, and telling you it's time to run away.

But here's the trick. *Anxiety is nothing more than you overestimating the likelihood of the worst-case scenario, multiplied by you underestimating your ability to cope with the outcome.* That's right, it really is as simple as overestimating one thing while underestimating another.

Take a few moments to really think about this. How often when you get anxious do you expect the absolute worst to happen? And when you imagine this scenario, is part of it generally you being unable to cope with the challenge at hand, you not being confident in your abilities to deal with it? I'd say that is a pretty standard panic thought pattern.

Realistically, how often, out of the thousands, even millions, of scenarios that have happened in your life, has the worst thing actually happened? I'm not saying it has never happened – we all have tragedies in our lives – but it doesn't happen often. So objectively speaking, what are the odds really? Also, how often, when a challenge occurs, have you failed so miserably that it was a total disaster? Probably not nearly enough for you to underestimate yourself as you are in this anxious thought pattern.

Remember this: you're more competent than you think. You don't rate yourself enough and your levels of confidence are so low that you don't believe you are capable of managing whatever unknown outcome might be placed in front of you. It feels as if it's too much, and you are too little. Luckily there are ways to manage this. The exercises at the end of this chapter are designed to help you build your confidence, so that in turn you can manage your anxiety.

How to build your confidence using MIND

The reality is that your confidence is built on whatever you believe to be true about yourself. So to build that confidence, see yourself for the diamond that you are and reframe failure, we will be using the MIND method.

Measurable success

My favourite moment with a client is when they tell me that other people have noticed a change in their attitude and confidence or have even noticed happiness and contentment radiating from them. I love this, the growth is real and noticeable. But the tragedy of being conditioned by our environment is that we rarely notice the changes in ourselves as we quickly become accustomed to our new world that we have created. The more confident version of ourselves becomes the new normal, the homeostatis, and this seamless adjustment makes us feel that we haven't progressed at all. This is a challenge, and I would be lying if I said that I don't appreciate it when my friends tell me I've changed for the better.

So, what should you do? You need to actively think about how you've changed. Think for instance about something that triggered you six months ago, and see how you respond to a similar stressor now. Can you see a difference?

I helped a woman who had suffered a particularly awful and traumatising car crash overcome her crippling fear of being in her car. This was something that would give her immense anxiety and debilitating panic attacks as a result of the trauma. We slowly started working on her confidence behind the wheel through exposure. Now, she tells me that every time she gets into her car she feels a sense of accomplishment, and she has got her confidence back for a task that in the past seemed gargantuan and awful.

This example illustrates a brilliant point. Think about the things that were once far too overwhelming to even contemplate, which are now the commonplace in your life. Maybe it's the first time you did a presentation in front of your colleagues, the first time you stood in a free weights area of a gym, the first time you gathered the courage to talk to the person you fancy and ask them out, the first time you spoke openly about your sexuality with someone you trust, the first time you danced with wild abandon in a club, and so on. There are countless examples of things we once found daunting that now feel like a breeze, or at least, manageable. That's real, measurable progress. And these are all examples of you behaving in an authentic and vulnerable way so others can see who you are and what you have become.

Intrinsic motivation

There is nothing like seeing the success that you have already achieved and using that to motivate you further. I encourage all of my clients to use a lived experience of overcoming a challenge and transform that moment into a small, repeatable statement for themselves. My personal example is 'always outnumbered, never outgunned'. That's the name of one of my favourite albums by one of my favourite bands. I listened to The Prodigy almost every day during my basic training. It's become the soundtrack to much of my life, and because both the music and that statement inspires so much confidence in me it fires me into action.

As a result, it's become a bit of a trigger for success, motivation, growth and brilliance in my life. I say it to myself ahead of intimidating events such as public speaking – most recently when I did a talk for MPs in Westminster about resilience. I might be outnumbered by them in the room, but I have my expertise, my life experiences, my academic knowledge, and I know what I bring to the table. I'm outnumbered, but not outgunned. This motivates me when I feel my confidence wavering, when I can feel myself struggle. I whisper it to myself as a trigger for my performance and it really works.

What's your statement? Take some time to find it. It could be a meaningful song lyric, something profound a caretaker once said to you, a book or movie quote, something from a speech by an important political figure, whatever works for you, as long as it triggers that intrinsic motivation inspires you into action.

Now, in the present

One thing I say very often to my clients in therapy is 'comparison is the thief of joy'. Comparing what you have, who you are, what you look like and what you do to someone else will do nothing for you. It will only bring you down and belittle you. It will break your motivation and send you back to the safety of your bed or couch and the belief that you never should have tried. It is a crushing thing to strive for something that you are extremely passionate about and to then see that someone else has done far better than you. 'Look at how much better they are than me, what am I even doing?' This can hurt your ego, so don't compare. It is easier said than done because it comes naturally to us to do so. But you need to remember you are looking at one tiny facet of a person and using that to make a judgement about this person's quality of life in general, while you don't know their whole story. Not to mention that this justifies a negative thought pattern about yourself. Remember the diamond analogy – we are all walking a unique path, with unique experiences.

We spoke of privilege at the start of the chapter, and this plays a huge role in our subjective achievements. Comparing your car that you work 14-hour days to be able afford to the Ferrari that someone drives around Knightsbridge in is not an accurate representation of your achievement. Belittling yourself and using someone else's achievements to undermine the value of yours shows nothing but your inability to see the bigger picture. You are comparing against something that does not have the exact same rules or starting point that you have. I play guitar (badly) and I sing (even worse) yet if I were to sit there and complain that I am not Jimi Hendrix or Adele, then I would never play. Moreover, it is not my job nor my sole function to play guitar and sing. I'm also writing, doing a university course, running my own business and of course, being a dad, which is most important of them all. Comparing yourself to others will just rob you of your joy and your confidence. It will seem as if attempting anything challenging is completely futile. And it's really not mindful. In the moment you achieve something, there is just you and your success, nothing else. Focus on your own achievements only and don't look to others. Stay in the moment, stay with yourself only and look at where you have come from and what you have achieved since.

Dream big

Bear with me because this is going to sound insane, but what if you just believed in yourself? I know this seems like a revolutionary thing to say, but what if you just did? What if you didn't doubt yourself? What if you genuinely believed that you were capable of achieving great things and you pursued them with confidence?

We all have that voice of fear, subconsciously generated, desperate to keep us safe. Our body produces a stress response when there is a behaviour, event or environment that makes us worry we might lose our position in the social hierarchy. We worry about how we may be perceived and what the social consequences may be. But why worry about the opinions of people who don't pay your bills or sleep in your bed? Moreover, the worst-case scenario you're imagining may very well never happen. Also, very importantly, if you don't ever challenge the status quo, if you don't push yourself out of your comfort zone, if you simply fail to do anything out of fear of judgement, you will inevitably become restless, bored and miserable.

Your subconscious really is a stroppy toddler if there ever was one. It doesn't like risk, but without taking risks you stay stagnant, you don't grow. That toddler will want to create a scene inside your head, but you can push forward unhindered, past its tantrum, once you understand what that fear really is.

Where would you be if you just went for what you wanted? Maybe this sounds easier than it is. But if you really can't manage to truly believe it, what if you just acted as if you believed in yourself? What if you walked with confidence and spoke with purpose from your chest? What if you looked people in the eye and shook their hand as if you meant it? What if you acted like the most confident version of yourself? What if you believed in the dream of all that you could be, and that all you really had to do was start acting like that person, with conviction, with belief and with confidence?

An old rugby coach once told me, 'Back yourself to the hilt, as no one else will.' He was right. If you just back yourself, you stand a far better chance of succeeding. It's what Rupert would do, so you should do it too. Claim that space. Most brilliant success stories simply start with a person with the gall to ask the question 'why not?' This person can easily be you. Dare to believe in the strength that you have because you do actually have it.

Exercises

Exercise 1: The diamond I am

One of my favourite motivational exercises is as follows. I ask a person to tell me who they are, what they love and hate, what their dreams and ambitions are, what they have achieved and what they are most proud of. Then I instruct them to think of themselves as a diamond, much as we did earlier in this chapter. Then I ask them their name. Rather than just saying for instance 'I'm James Elliot', the instruction here is to instead say something like, 'I am *the* James Elliot, the one and only, the authentic individual, the man pushing forward towards his own goals, doing what only he can do, in only the way he can do it, and understanding that this is what makes him the rare and precious diamond he is.' Sounds silly, but it works. It really, really works. From Olympians, to Special Forces, to people with all types of troubles, the same is true for everyone who comes to me as a client: the most important part is that they appreciate themselves, and that they verbally enforce this to themselves. Give it a go and repeat the exercise every time you feel the need to boost your Confidence pillar.

Exercise 2: Write a letter to yourself

As discussed earlier when we talked about impostor syndrome, dismissing your brilliance is common. There are several reasons for this, among them the cultural implication that being really proud of who you are is often mislabelled as 'arrogance'. But it isn't at all, and the reason people are so willing to quickly label you as 'arrogant' for being proud of something you've done is because your achievement might be a reflection of their lack of success. There is a wonderful line from the series *Blackadder Goes Forth* (the one in the trenches with the incredibly powerful ending), where Lieutenant George reveals some unbelievably good paintings that he has made, and Blackadder says, 'But, George, these are brilliant, why didn't you tell us about these before?' George responds, 'Well, you know, one doesn't like to blow one's own trumpet' and Blackadder says, 'You might at least have told us you had a trumpet.' This quick wit is a nod to this conditioning, which is a particularly British thing. We undersell ourselves, don't consider our achievements and growth, and that conditioning is most prevalent in our own heads.

To get you started on unlearning this conditioning, write a letter to your younger self. I love giving clients this exercise as homework because it plays a key role in building confidence and brings them closure. You need to pick a point in time when you felt at your lowest, broken and beaten by life, when you couldn't see a way out. Now, be the person you needed in your life at that time. Tell your younger self about who they will become. Tell them about all the brilliant things that have happened, the things you've achieved, the stumbling blocks, the fulfilled dreams and the missed chances, the ups and downs, victories and losses. Tell them how this shaped who you are now, and that all of it led to this person, this diamond, that you are today.

Write with detail, gusto, momentum and authenticity. Don't care about spelling or grammar, just write what's in your heart. This can be a very emotional process. It can be triggering, you could cry or be angry or remorseful, but ultimately, you will be proud of yourself at the end.

The point of this exercise is for you to realise that you are so much more than how you perceive yourself. You are more than your trauma, your pain and suffering, your loss, your regrets. That is not who you are. Instead, see the brilliance that's inside you. You are a force of nature. You are designed to grow, to fill a space and to explore. Tell your younger self this, and see what happens.

Exercise 3: Thought court

As mentioned earlier in this chapter, we can define anxiety as a simple mathematic equation of overestimating the likelihood of the worst-case scenario multiplied by underestimating our ability to cope. This really comes down to confidence, because as discussed earlier, we tend to underestimate ourselves regularly.

The key here is to learn to look at this equation as objectively as possible. Instead of the worst thing that could happen, let's look at the likeliest thing to happen. I would like to introduce you to an exercise that I call 'the thought court'. The thought court is an imaginary court of justice that you create in your mind. In this court, I would like you to put your negative thought processes on trial and place yourself in the role of the lawyer trying to convince a jury that the negative thought is incorrect. You need to be as objective and persuasive as possible in your role in the court, otherwise you will not convince the jury, so you need to come up with real, factual and tangible evidence to persuade them. So, in this situation that you're facing, what is the actual, real-life, most likely thing that is going to happen? Doesn't this scenario actually make more sense than the doom scenario you were picturing before? Isn't it objectively more likely to happen this way instead? Then, think about your own abilities. Isn't there plenty of evidence already to show that you are actually quite capable of dealing with whatever the likeliest outcome is? Haven't you proven yourself already through countless other challenges to be tough, resilient and competent? So why would it be different this time?

You will soon realise that the previous scenario you were fearing is not very likely at all to happen, and that you are in any case completely able to deal with whatever will come at you. Case dismissed.

Summary

Developing confidence is a really difficult thing to do. What it means to each of us is so subjective, and our negative internal dialogue can rip it down. We all have unique experiences and circumstances in life, and because life is not a level playing field, building confidence isn't either. But for you to be resilient, you need to have confidence. Confidence will help you face challenges and handle adversity. It will help turn surviving into thriving. We need to believe that we have the capabilities to manage whatever is thrown at us. We need to believe in who we are, in what we are – flaws included. No diamond is perfect, and neither are you. But a diamond's flaws and inclusions are what make it unique, and it is beautiful because of it, not in spite of it. See yourself as a whole, and celebrate all your qualities.

You can develop your confidence by interrogating your negative thought patterns, celebrating your wins, never comparing your achievements to others, and actively practising self-belief. Keep telling yourself you are capable, and the more you do so, the more you will start believing in yourself, and the more resilient you will become.

CHAPTER TWO

Emotional Intelligence

What you can expect to learn from this chapter:

- What emotions are.
- Why we have them.
- How we can manage them.
- What emotions teach us about ourselves.
- How we can grow from them.

I'm five years old, and I am in the bathroom of my mum and dad's home. I'm curled up as small as I can be, right behind the toilet, wedged somehow in that tiny space behind there. I can hear my mum and dad screaming on the other side of the door. Her back is against the locked door. It's one of those mahogany doors, but it's not real wood, it's like thick cardboard that's been covered in laminate. I remember this door as if it was yesterday.

She is screaming at me to not open the door. I know he's punching her. I can hear the thuds and the resultant screams of pain. I can hear her being slammed against the wall. I can hear the noise that people make when they are punched in the stomach, that 'ugh' noise. He is hitting her there and in her privates. He would do this to not leave bruises on her face. I can hear my sister screaming, I can hear my mum screaming. I am in a completely catatonic state of fear, helpless and submissive, I am just five and I am in such a state of shock I cannot breathe.

*

As I sit here, writing the introduction to this chapter, I once again feel tears filling my eyes. This would happen a lot. My biological dad was a violent man. My mum managed to escape later, but I didn't, and I remember being so scared of being at his house, of being near him and having no choice but to stay.

When I was 28, I went and met him after years of no contact. As a child, he had been abusive and vile to me, my mum and my sister. He would enjoy seeing the burden he put on me with his treatment of us. I can still see his sneer, and I imagine he thought that to hurt a little boy, his own son, to dominate someone in such a way that they spend their entire lives recovering from it, would in some way validate his own strength.

As I stood in the staff room in the place where he worked, making a cup of tea for myself, not knowing what reaction my unannounced arrival would bring, I found a feeling of peace. In the doorway stood an old man, frail yet slightly overweight, with grey hair that was still thick and full (perhaps one good thing I might inherit from him?). His skin looked atrocious, as if it was hanging off his body, drooping and sagging, aged and colourless. It was clear from taking one look at this man that he was slowly dying. It was as if he was decomposing in front of me while still alive.

This is what years of smoking, drink and drugs do to you. He was once enormous and intimidating – not just because I was a child at the time but because he was objectively so. He would love to have read that actually, that this was how I saw him. Even as an adult I found him terrifying. He was slightly hunched and clutching an elaborate walking stick – he would have thought that this added to his 'gangster' appearance. He was obsessed with gangsters, and it was the reason he became a drug dealer. He looked me up and down, his faded eyes lit up, and yellow, rotting teeth appeared as he, so predictably, sneered: 'See? I don't regret what I did to you boy. I have made you strong.'

I felt a huge release hearing those words come out of his mouth. Let me be clear: not because he now perceived me as strong. I don't care for that. It's because it became clear to me that he lacked the strength, the courage, the emotional intelligence to say, 'I am sorry'. He never could. He couldn't say this to anyone, because it was then and always would be about *his* insecurity. In that moment, I discovered something I hadn't realised my entire life. That it was *him*. It wasn't me: the pain had been his all along. The anger I was exposed to was his, not mine, to carry. The self-loathing from years of abuse was his to hold and his alone. I had been carrying his pain for him, and in that moment I knew I deserved better for me, from me.

This is the basis of emotional intelligence. It's the knowledge that you deserve better than your instinctual reaction of fear, and the damaging, life-changing decisions those negative reactions will bring. Emotional intelligence is the ability to recognise and understand your own emotional reactions, to know your strengths and limitations. It is the ability to regulate your emotional reactions, to see them as they are and not to be overtaken by them. Emotional intelligence is empathy, and the understanding that your perspective is a reflection of you, your upbringing, your beliefs, your decisions and your mistakes.

I don't hide my mental health; I have had serious struggles. I can browse my mental health diagnoses and issues throughout my life on my NHS app, and I can view my life experiences in a few simple lines:

- Childhood depression (significant)
- Physical childhood abuse (significant)
- Mixed anxiety and depressive disorder (significant and ongoing)

- Psychiatric disorder (related to a history of stress, poor mental health and anxiety).

I can read over these diagnoses, these events that have shaped so much of me now as an adult, stretching from my childhood to only a few months ago. I can relay incidents and memories from my life that have triggered huge emotional responses within me. I remember the violence and the anger that I used to protect myself, how being triggered would involve alcohol and rage and anything I could do to mask the pain, the suffering, the inability to like or even love myself. I remember the hatred for myself and for those who had mistreated and abused me and let me down. I developed this anger as a young child and cultivated it as a teenager before allowing it to consume me whole. I carried with me a burden that got increasingly heavy, that weighed me down, growing up under the boot of an abusive, drug-dealing father, suffering around those who also suffered from him, developing coping mechanisms for his behaviour that meant isolating myself, that meant fear.

Like a lot of people who suffer with their mental health, I have been both a victim and a perpetrator of violent crime. I have a criminal record; I had been arrested for violence and drunk and disorderly behaviour multiple times before my 21st birthday. In my life, I have joined the Army and become part of the incredible Airborne Forces at 18, served my country on operations in Afghanistan, become a low-level (referring to height of parachute not character!) tactical parachuting instructor, broken five world records, lost my mind and found it, become a dad, loved and lost, and finally found a version of myself that I can build with. I have learned to cry, to feel what I believe a version of normality must be. I have learned how to study and grow, and how to weaponise my experiences into something useful for those who approach me for help, to arm them against the same demons and fears that plagued me. I have qualified as a psychotherapist and counsellor specialised in advanced CBT methods, I am (at time of writing) studying at King's College London for my master's in war and psychiatry. I have been medicated for my poor mental health and cycled off (this is the gradual reduction in dosage, a very important part of the eventual 'coming off' of the medication) the antidepressant, citalopram. I have failed far more than I have succeeded, but with each failure comes a lesson, and with each lesson comes the opportunity to try again, this time wiser and better prepared.

Emotional intelligence is a superpower. It is your strength, it is your control, it is true self-love and respect. But what is emotional intelligence, actually? If you ask a hundred people what their definition of emotional intelligence is you'll get a hundred different answers, and there is an interesting split with my clients when I ask them what it means. Some say that it's being aware of your emotions and regulating them, and others define it as the awareness of other people's emotions and the effect that you have on them. I would agree with both, as well as the definitions I gave earlier. It's all of these things. If I had to define it for myself, I would break it down into the following five points:

1. Self-awareness: Being aware of your feelings and how they translate into emotions. It's how your body is physiologically responding and what that means emotionally.
2. Emotional regulation: The ability to manage your emotions, not be negatively swayed by them, and control them rather than let them control you.
3. Empathy: Being empathetic towards both yourself and your very human reactions, as well as understanding other people's emotions and responses. It's knowing that we're all struggling and trying to do our best.

4. Social awareness: Being aware of how your attitudes, behaviours and beliefs affect other people and the emotional state this puts others in.

5. Motivation: The motivation, once you've mastered points 1–4, to actually act on them, put your pride aside and make the changes needed to improve your emotional intelligence. Pride is the devil.

The ability to build your emotional intelligence is, in my opinion, the single most important human quality that exists. Even as I write this book now, I find myself welling up sometimes at how human and flawed I am, and that I am all the wiser because of it.

I am struck by the sudden absurd realisation that my dad was right. Not in the way that he meant of course. Not in any forgivable way, not in a way that excuses anything he did, but the sense that he has allowed me to help so many other people with their emotional intelligence. He did make me strong after all, but he did it by making me vulnerable and forcing me to process my hurt, hate and pain. He did make me strong, just not in the way he intended. He wanted me to be subservient and scared of him. But I chose a different path.

Eventually, I did develop that empathy and compassion. Like all of us, I suffer from my own ridiculousness and vulnerability. I am human, but I am *so* human that I'm aware of it. In fact, I'm proud of my humanity.

For all those who may read this and knew the James Elliot from another time, another place and another version of me, I am truly sorry if I have ever projected this hate and self-loathing onto you. If we ever meet again, I will have to reintroduce myself, because cultivating emotional intelligence didn't just change me, it tore me down and rebuilt me.

Ask anyone, including yourself, what your biggest flaws are. If they or you don't know, then your single biggest flaw is this: a lack of emotional intelligence. But know you do deserve better. Emotional intelligence isn't just about knowing what your flaws are, but also knowing you deserve better.

Here is how you grow your emotional intelligence.

Understanding our emotions

Emotions are incredible things. They are intrinsically built into us and almost impossible to accurately predict. People even have the ability to react to things in completely opposite ways. The study conducted by Thomas Bouchard and his team in 1990 called 'Sources of Human Psychological Differences: The Minnesota Study of Twins Reared Apart', examined twins and how their behaviours were similar and how they varied depending on the environment in which they were raised.[1] The study found that twins brought up in the same environment with similar childhood experiences showed different emotional responses and emotional expressions to stimuli.

This shows us that emotional responses really are subconscious. When we then consider that roughly 80 per cent of our decision-making process is subconscious, we can see how important it is to understand our emotions.[2]

As you might remember from earlier on in this book, psychologists Ekman and Friesen defined six basic emotions all humans experience: happiness, sadness, fear, disgust, anger and surprise.[3] Most of this chapter will focus on one of these emotions, which is fear. Fear is a huge motivator for behaviour. It can be observed in many different forms and is triggered by many different things.

We'll first look at the neurological process of a fearful reaction, and how this affects our resilience. Fear will convince you of the greatest lie of them all: that you are incapable of managing the adversity you're facing, that you must immediately quit and run away. This is the internal cave person that lives in all of us, wanting us to find safety immediately and never even think about risking anything ever again. Fear is the enemy of mental resilience. Let's talk about how we can slay this enemy.

Going back to the example we looked at the beginning of this book, let's imagine you're driving to work. You feel relaxed, but suddenly a car swerves into your lane in front of you, erratic and desperate, speeding, and millimetres away from hitting you. You'll likely slam on the brakes, take in a breath sharply, grip the steering wheel, and feel a freezing cold in your gut while your body tenses up. This is what we are going to call stage 1: the physiology of an emotional trigger.

Then comes the anger, a huge, overwhelming desire to scream and shout at the irresponsibility of the driver in front of you. It's the rage that you feel and the anger that clouds your judgement for a few moments, and as the driver inevitably disappears behind the horizon, you begin to relax and recover yourself. This is stage 2: the psychological response.

After a few moments, you can feel yourself returning to homeostasis. Perhaps you realise that Oasis is playing on the radio (the greatest band of all time, fight me) and that everything is actually fine. You take a breath, and if your reaction to this driver has been particularly explosive, you might feel a sense of embarrassment. If your kids are in the car, you may even feel the need apologise and say, 'Sorry about that sweetheart, silly drivers. Don't swear like that though; do as I say, not as I do!' This is stage 3: the control stage.

Stage 1: The physiology of an emotional response

Human beings crave a state of homeostasis, which means our hormones are in balance and this gives us a feeling of peace. We like the odd bit of manageable stress, which is why we get on rollercoasters and play sports, as it gives us a feeling of excitement. But a car swerving in front of us, nearly causing us a fiery death, is a bit too much. We perceive this as a danger (which it is of course) and we respond accordingly.

The perception of threat starts with observation. We see the car swerve into our view, and this observation travels from our eyes via the optic nerve to the thalamus. This part of the brain turns sensory data into information, so that our brain can choose the appropriate reaction. This information is then passed to the amygdala, which interprets this information as a danger, and generates the emotion of fear. The amygdala then communicates with the hippocampus, and basically asks, 'What do we do?' The hippocampus, as our emotional memory bank, has stored everything we've experienced in our subconscious, and this information is ready to be accessed when our amygdala is scanning for danger and wants to know what the appropriate response is based on previous experiences. While this is happening, the amygdala also releases a huge rush of hormones, including cortisol (a stress hormone) and adrenaline (the 'kickstart everything' hormone), which functions as the body's early warning system.

Adrenaline and cortisol bolt out like greyhounds from their cages and flood the body immediately. This is when you feel your heart rate quickening as the pressure mounts to get blood pumped around the body, with your muscles tensing and preparing to be able to quickly flee or fight. Perhaps you experience a sharp intake of breath as the airways in your lungs are suddenly pulled open. Your pupils dilate – often giving the illusion that time is moving slowly – letting in as much light as possible to see the threat more clearly.

The amygdala gets information from the hippocampus, which is saying, 'Slam on the brakes!' or, 'Swerve out of the way!', and we act accordingly. The instruction it picks is based on your emotional memory. Your hippocampus grows, learns and develops mostly during your childhood, which is why our formative experiences are so important to how we emotionally respond as adults. In this example, if your parents were rally car drivers and you spent a big part of your childhood in race cars, your response to the swerving driver might be a lot more skilled and controlled than if you are a new driver who has only been on the road for a few weeks. Our emotional reactions are based on what we have previously experienced.

Our reactions stem from an intrinsic desire for safety. It has now overwhelmed us, and we are presenting behaviours that ensure our survival. Fear has gripped us and created a huge physiological response. It varies from person to person, but overwhelmingly, the consensus seems to be that most people feel this fear in their stomach. This is the flight, fight or freeze mode activation. The body prepares itself for survival at the sudden appearance of a threat, and it is overwhelming.

This physiological response continues until the threat has been fled from, confronted, or avoided (again, flight, fight or freeze). When the threat is over, the brain acknowledges this and dials back our crisis hormone levels, and eventually our body returns to a state of homeostasis. The stress has been managed, and we are no longer under any threat. The coping mechanism that we used to deal with that stress embeds itself firmly in the hippocampus for future reference. This whole process is incredible. It was designed to keep us safe during the prehistoric era of our human existence, long before the comfort and luxury and minor inconveniences that we deal with today.

It is essential for the development of emotional intelligence that you listen to your body and its responses. Your subconscious is designed to keep you safe and is constantly chatting to you. The problem is that, in this age of constant stimulation, actually hearing it can be difficult. Also, as mentioned previously, society has evolved faster than our bodies, and the emotional response we once had to seeing a venomous snake, we now have to meeting a challenging deadline, speaking in public or whatever makes us scared.

Regardless, the ability to know what your body is trying to tell you is such a superpower. Your subconscious mind doesn't speak to you the same way your conscious mind would – it would simply be far too loud and overwhelming – so your subconscious communicates with you through your nervous system instead.

Trust your body to tell you that something isn't safe or is too stressful. The tightening of your chest, the butterflies in your stomach, cold feet and hands, headaches, digestive discomfort, there are hundreds of subjective ways the subconscious tries to communicate with us. Of course, if you suffer from an anxiety disorder, post-traumatic stress disorder (PTSD) or panic attacks, your body's signalling might be a bit off and it will perhaps perceive threats where there are none. Still, if you do have a very intense response to a certain stimuli or trigger, it's worth trying to calm your body down as much as you can and bring it back to homeostasis, as a calm body will lead to a calmer mind. There are exercises at the end of this chapter to help you with this.

Stage 2: The psychological response

The psychology of a stress response is truly fascinating. This is effectively how we *think* about stress and our responses to it. While our subconscious regulates the body and the physical feelings we get, it's important to note that this response can be reduced and managed by how we think and what we actively choose to do.

Our emotional reactions, meaning here the release of neuro-chemicals in our bodies, are not something we can take ownership of. Our subconscious reacts incredibly quickly, and we have evolved to have these physiological reactions quickly in order to survive. But how we choose to display these emotions is absolutely something that we can take ownership of. In fact, in order to cultivate mental resilience, we *must* take ownership of this. We must learn this control and this self-compassion because the capability for higher thought is a human superpower. Yet we are so quick to put the responsibility elsewhere, to blame it on our temper, the people around us, our society and our beliefs. The psychological response dictates our behaviour and, once mastered, it will set you free.

Let's get back to the example of the car swerving in front of you. What's noteworthy here is that this scenario of course does not end when the threat is gone. Even the most stoic human on the planet would look incredibly bizarre not batting an eyelid after having gone through a life-saving physiological response, skidding to a halt moments from death. What's actually more likely to happen is that the moment your car comes to a halt, you want to scream, shout and swear. Your anger explodes, your thoughts turn from Oasis on the radio to 'HOW DARE THEY DO THAT TO ME!' The rage is real, and your anger generates furious language spewing from your mouth, you scream, perhaps you punch the steering wheel and make a few sordid hand gestures. To put it simply, you have lost the plot. The emotional subconscious has successfully commandeered your conscious thought.

All fully functioning humans have two distinct parts of the decision-making process: the subconscious and the conscious. The subconscious is in charge of the body, our emotional reactions that look after our basic needs, such as food, shelter and safety. Our subconscious will generate emotional reactions by changing how our body feels, so that our conscious mind makes decisions to meet these basic needs. Because it would be too noisy if our subconscious communicated to us the same way that our conscious mind does, through internal dialogue, the subconscious talks to us through our body, and it inspires a response from us consciously.

Once the amygdala is ignited by a perception of threat and fear, it communicates this with the conscious mind, and we begin to 'think angry'. You're now conscious of the thought that the swerving driver so dangerously nearly caused your death, which causes anger and frustration. Your behaviour is a representation of that, hence the swearing and the hand gestures and punching the steering wheel. You throw caution to the wind, and you explode. It's what we call 'in the heat of the moment': you just don't care about the consequences of your behaviour in that moment. This happens because your emotional memory bank, the hippocampus, has been taught that this is the behaviour required to survive. And when you believe you've successfully managed a threat, this brings an instantaneous release of dopamine, our reward hormone (more on this in the Physical Health chapter).

Here's the super interesting part: what were you emotionally reacting to in this incident of road rage? It was fear, wasn't it? It was fear for yourself, your safety, your life. The behaviours you then display that lead to self-preservation are absolutely essential. But the screaming and shouting? This is fear turning into anger. Your life is no longer at risk, and if you are to accurately examine the thoughts you had and the language you used in this moment, they are concerned with the dehumanisation, belittling and threat to you as an individual. This is a fear of societal judgement, a fear of loss of a position of authority. And with this, you achieve *nothing*. The driver has already gone. They can't hear you. Your shouts are aimed at someone who is no longer there. All this says to me is that you allow fear to make you behave in an irrational way, which leads to no outcome, and you will later regret it.

Just to be clear, I'm not in any way judging you for thinking, *I do that*. I have done that too. I've responded this way in traffic jams, at work, on nights out where there would sometimes even be physical altercations. And how does this reflect on me? There's no strength there, no stoicism, no leadership, no compassion and no real power in this response. Please don't buy into the false narrative often portrayed in social media that power comes from dominating another person verbally or physically. Real power comes from control, not from neurotic volatility. Mental resilience therefore requires emotional intelligence. In these moments, if you aren't aware of why you are feeling the way you are, if you get overwhelmed and are easily overpowered by your emotions, then quite simply every single time you face adversity, you will turn away.

Stage 3: The control stage

Your body will physiologically respond far quicker than you can ever cognitively piece together exactly what is happening. Consider the double take when you think you have seen something threatening. You glance, there is a rush of cortisol, and you glance again, just to realise that it was nothing there all along. That is your body reacting faster than your mind can respond. It is survival, ancient and essential. Let us use that to our advantage. There are lots of times I talk about the weaponisation of certain processes, and this is one of those instances. The physiological response to an apparent stressor can be manipulated to our advantage if we treat it like an advanced warning system.

We used to have this terrifying Major in basic training who was originally a private soldier and worked his way up the ranks, serving in every major military conflict of modern times. I swear if you squint, you can see him in the background of the Bayeux Tapestry. He had these proper menacing-looking dogs, which acted as if they were at the Somme with him. The dogs would patrol in front of the Major as he walked, probably hoping to be fed the remains of a recruit who annoyed him. When the dogs were spotted in the corridor, soldiers would panic. They'd nervously whisper, 'He's here!' and people would instantly make preparations for the Major's arrival.

The more this happened, the better we became at it and the more prepared and ready for the fearful reactions the Major would try to evoke in us. The dogs are a perfect metaphor for emotional regulation. They are a representation of our physiological responses

– the butterflies in our stomach, the racing heart rate – and feelings that we get prior to a psychological response to fear. In the same way, we would prepare and manage his arrival at the appearance of his dogs, so must you learn to manage your emotions at the arrival of your physiological feelings. To help you with this, I have developed the FOCUS method of control. Allow me to explain.

FOCUS

F = FEEL. Feel your physiological responses. The more aware you are of your body, the more in tune you are with what your subconscious is trying to tell you. It's almost constantly talking to you, and the more able you become at understanding it, the better you will become at responding effectively to it. What are you feeling, physically? Is it a tightness in your chest, a flutter in your stomach, are you hot or cold, is your heart rate rising? Be aware of your body's alert system to become in tune with your body. You have to really pay attention to what you're feeling in order to catch that emotional response early.

O = OBSERVE. Now observe that emotion. What is the source of it? The key is not to ask yourself why you are feeling a certain way, but rather, why your subconscious is choosing to feel this way. Remember that emotions are effectively generated by a subconscious conversation with your emotional memory bank, the hippocampus. The hippocampus is reminding you of something that is creating that response. Consider what that memory is. Is it something from your childhood? A past relationship? Emotions have a source, so what is the source of this? Then consider your emotions like an unwelcome visitor, like a person who has just turned up at your house without invitation. See the house as a representation of your mind and the visitor as the emotion coming in. It is normal to feel that they are unwanted and rude for just turning up and to feel slightly indignant that they have intruded at all. But we don't *become* the visitor. We just simply observe them and wait for them to pleasantly leave.

C = CONTROL. Now control that emotion. There are lots and lots of very valid and brilliant ways of doing this. At this point, the emotion is likely to still be playing havoc in your body. It's coursing through your nervous system, and even though you're aware of this, that might not stop you from acting on it. It doesn't necessarily stop you from quitting, from lashing out, from chasing after that car driver, from screaming, or sending an irrational email/Slack DM/WhatsApp/Tinder/Hinge/Bumble/Insta DM/ Twitter DM/Facebook Message/TikTok Message (maybe we should reduce the number of ways that we can communicate?). You still want to act irrationally, to express your anger, fuelled by adrenaline and cortisol. And moments after, you regret it.

So instead, focus your attention. Take a couple of deep breaths. Why is it so upsetting that this person has done this to you? Will there be any positive outcome from you responding this way? Take a moment to think about yourself, the version of you 15 minutes, an hour and a day from now. Will you still want to react this way, or is this just a way for you to blow off steam, to get the tension out, to lash out at someone who has crossed you? Will you regret acting this way later on? Is reacting this way in line with your core values? Somewhere between the stressful event happening and your reaction to it, there is a space where you can consider this. And within that space is a choice, and this choice leads to freedom. At the end of this chapter, there is a breathing exercise that will help you with managing this even better.

U = USE. Use this simple question, 'What advice would I give to someone else in this exact same situation?' I usually think about my daughter in this scenario, but you can pick whoever you like. Often when people find themselves being challenged, their immediate thought pattern is that they're incompetent and somehow are presented with evidence that they've been doing something incorrectly or inefficiently. From a skewed and misinformed perspective people will blame themselves, become defensive or even subtly aggressive. Asking this question removes the hypercritical view we often have of ourselves and shifts the focus to asking yourself this question as if you are your own friend. Our internal dialogue is often horrible, critical and unnecessarily harsh. Would you ever talk to a friend the way you talk to yourself? Of course not! So turn this around. What advice you would give to someone you genuinely care about and love, a person you want the best for, who you want to nurture, grow and support? This is the person that you should be thinking of. What advice would you give them in your exact same situation? Now give that advice to yourself.

Once you have your physiological response to a stressor under control, you have calmed your body, and your amygdala's influence on your prefrontal cortex has been managed, it leaves you a space. This is the space to make a decision, and within that space, make the decision to treat yourself compassionately. If someone you care about was in the exact same position as you – say, they were struggling with their workload, their fitness goals, their terrible boss, their relationship – what advice would you give them? I guarantee that very, very few would say, 'Suck it up. We all have it bad.' The vast majority would offer careful, gentle and balanced solutions that ensure longevity, that ensure growth and support of the person we care about, that help that person to keep going. This is what you must do for yourself.

S = SUCCEED. 'It's not what happens to you, but how you react to it that matters,' so said Epictetus. Cheers, big guy! This ancient Greek philosopher, who was born into slavery, was entirely correct. Things can and do often go south and fall apart. There is a classic (and clichéd) and somewhat painful Army saying, 'No plan survives first contact'. It's absolutely true. Thing rarely ever go as we expect them to. Humans are incredibly difficult to predict, and since we spend most of our life navigating them, this means our lives are too. And life is ever changing. Darwin noted this – he pointed out that the species that remains at the top of its food chain is not the most vicious, nor the most poisonous: it is the one most adaptable to change. So, once the stressor has passed, once your physical reaction has calmed down, you've observed your emotions, found the space to act in a positive and constructive way, look back on what has happened. Can you look back and say you managed that the best way you could have? Do you regret how you acted? Was your behaviour in line with your values? Did you treat yourself kindly in this moment? If you answer yes to these questions, then you managed yourself successfully. Now bank that. Remember it for future reference, and draw from it when the next challenge, inevitably, comes.

If you learn to use FOCUS you will find yourself making far more effective decisions that will push you towards your subjective sense of fulfilment. The ability to stay calm when everyone else is losing their mind is a superpower. You can become a rock for people when they need it. You can stop yourself from throwing away and sacrificing things that are important to you in the heat of the moment for immediate release. You will gain the ability to stay calm and controlled, and this is what will help you grow your mental resilience. The more often you repeat FOCUS, the more innate it will become. And soon, when a challenge arises you will instinctively ask yourself, 'Why am I choosing to act this way? What will I gain?', rather than flying off the handle.

It's worth noting here that, when faced with adversity, most people undermine themselves. They throw their self-regard away and are insistent that they are incapable. I have already discussed talking to yourself as a friend, but there's another piece of the puzzle.

Whenever we're faced with something new and daunting, most of us are actually incapable or even useless at first. Look back on the first day in your job – did you even know half the stuff you know now? Of course not. If you're a parent, do you look back on your early parenting days and think, *That guy/girl has no idea what they're doing*? Of course you do!

Most of us have no idea what on earth we are doing half the time, while we seem to think that everyone around us does. Some of us might even feel like imposters, just barely stumbling through life, secretly feeling that we don't belong in our job, our university course, our gym, our friendship circles even.

The big difference, in all my experience of observing human behaviour, and working with so many brilliant people (who incidentally, often do not see themselves as such), is that between success and failure is the ability to hold on for just one more day. And a huge amount of emotional resilience centres around how you communicate with yourself. If you consider yourself to be resilient, if you tell yourself that you are and say that you are to others, then you're more likely to hang on for another day. If you say it, you are far more likely to become it.

As much as I'd like to say something different here, there really is no self-help book that will change you, no podcast you can listen to that will make your problems go away, no seminar you can sit in, no therapist who can change your world. They can help, of course, and set you on a path, but the only person on this planet who can bring about the great change that you crave is *you*. I've given you something to practise, a skill which is a shield against the adversity in the world: FOCUS. You can use this tool to build that pillar of emotional intelligence. The more you start to understand your own reactions, the more educated and informed you will become on who you are and what has happened throughout your life that has affected you. And the more you develop this sense of self, the more understanding you will become of others and their reactions too.

Trauma and emotional intelligence

Trauma is where the plot thickens. The definition for trauma is quite broad, but generally this refers to experiences that are very distressing or disturbing. Trauma is relative, and not necessarily defined by the event so much as a person's subjective experience of that event.

Traumatic memories are deeply embedded in our hippocampus, which subconsciously assists us with our decision making. The hippocampus also helps us decide whether a situation, context, person or environment is a cause for concern, and this will dictate how our emotional subconscious chooses to respond to this concern and how we consciously respond to it. So what happens when what's imbedded in there is deeply traumatic, and how does that play a role in our behaviour?

Deeply traumatic experiences, particularly those experienced in childhood, can have a wildly detrimental effect on our perspective and behaviour as adults. As I said, trauma is subjective, and people can respond quite differently to experiencing the same event. Consider this hypothetical example of two twin sons of an alcoholic father. Due to his traumatic upbringing, one of the sons might become aggressive, violent, foul mouthed, perhaps even an alcoholic himself. He might hurt people around him and might not think twice before savaging those more vulnerable than himself. The other might actually grow up to be a successful man, perhaps a philanthropist and a caring member of society. He might take great fulfilment from his life, be educated and interested in the world around him.

If you were to ask either twin why they are the way they are, they will both give the same answer: 'Because my father was an alcoholic'. This is a very simplistic example, and kind of a false dichotomy as people are nuanced and much more complex than this. But I've seen versions of this story happen in my practice – some of us absorb and repeat the challenges of our childhoods, while others reject them and protect others from their harmful effects.

The moment we exit the womb, we begin absorbing the world around us. How we interact with others, how we experience and relate to pain and pleasure, love and anger, all of this we learn by observing the world around us and by being shown certain behaviours. Have you ever caught yourself saying or thinking, 'Oh my god! I am turning into my mum/dad!'? Have you noticed that you are becoming more and more like them and their behaviours as a parent yourself? That is this exact process in action. You're very likely projecting your own experiences of childhood onto your own children, and this can be very difficult to manage.

And what we are taught by our parents, and what we teach our children in return is the foundation on which our pillars are originally built. Nurtured and supported children, growing up in positive environments with manageable challenges, knowing and feeling that they are supported, are far more likely to be resilient children. And in contrast, children who don't feel nurtured, who are neglected emotionally and face challenges kids shouldn't have to face, are far more likely to be less resilient.

Diving deeper into trauma, it's interesting to note that how traumatic an experience is considered to be has a lot to do with how much control the person experiencing it has in that situation, when they feel their survival is being threatened. What we can observe with most traumatic experiences is that the person experiencing the traumatic events often has very little control, or feels that they have very little control, over a distressing situation. This is why we say it's not the event as much as the experience of that event that causes the trauma. This may seem bizarre, but let's examine that in more detail.

In a study done by Bessel van der Kolk, children who had witnessed the events of 9/11 were asked to draw their interpretation of the event, and what happened next was very interesting.[4] Most children started drawing ways for the victims to survive, even in moments of great peril. They had drawn people getting piggybacks from dinosaurs, jumping onto enormous trampolines, being picked up by massive birds, and so on.

This illustrates how we naturally search for survival, and when we cannot generate that source of survival, that's when we can become traumatised. Survivors of sexual assault, stripped of their power, hurt and demeaned beyond all reasoning, do not play a role in their own survival when the assault happens and are traumatised. Soldiers on the receiving end of incoming enemy mortars, who curl into a ball in the ground and beg for swift death, do not play a role in their own survival in that moment and suffer trauma as a result.

It is in this state of total helplessness and inability to create our own reprise that we develop PTSD. This is explained in great detail by the incredible writings of Bessel van der Kolk in *The Body Keeps the Score*.[1] If you haven't read it yet, you must! It will tell you everything you need to know about trauma.

So, what happens when the hippocampus stores a belief that you are incapable of facilitating your own survival when faced with danger? We start to see volatile reactions to external stimuli that either consciously or subconsciously remind us of that event. We see seemingly irrational explosions of anger, distancing and disassociation; we see overwhelming fear and panic attacks. Why does this happen? In that moment, even if you're not actually in danger, your brain is convinced that you are and that your safety is being threatened and that, because you aren't in control of the situation, you don't have the capabilities to survive. Having a hair-trigger alarm system like this can cause great difficulty in leading a fulfilling life. People with PTSD can seem easily scared and overwhelmed by seemingly everyday events. It's difficult for those who do not have that trauma to understand why people can react the way they do. This is why empathy and compassion are so important – just because you don't understand someone's fearful reaction to something, they are still feeling that emotion and need empathy and compassion to get through it.

Trauma is stored in our brains differently from regular memories. Memory is a very complicated subject, but essentially we have two types of memories, implicit and explicit. Implicit memories are 'non-verbal' (meaning they're difficult to describe in words) and are used unconsciously. They allow you to perform tasks without thinking, such as riding a bike, typing on a computer keyboard, playing an instrument. Explicit memory is conscious and intentional recollection of information. This is how you recall facts, for instance what the capital of Spain is or what you had for lunch yesterday.

Contrary to most memories, trauma is often stored in our implicit memory. This is problematic, because implicit memory does not understand context. We see, for instance, that some survivors of sexual assault feel huge, overwhelming fear when someone else makes physical contact. The body has stored a memory that physical contact is dangerous and something to be afraid of, and so it has a fear reaction. But this is out of context, because the hippocampus fails to recognise that they are not in the same environment, place or time that they were when the assault happened.

Some victims of trauma, especially when this happened in childhood, repeat the traumatising behaviour that was modelled to them by caregivers.

Early on in this book I mentioned that children imitate their caregivers' behaviours and coping mechanisms. This is true, but as we grow into adulthood there is a choice. Now think again about the hypothetical example of the twin brothers raised by their alcoholic father. As said previously, one twin has resigned themselves to live out the behaviour modelled to them in their childhood. They have deeply imbedded the trauma of living in constant fear and stress with an abusive or neglectful parent in their hippocampus. They repeat the coping mechanisms shown to them by their father, and they're likely to turn to drink. The other twin, however, actively rejects this behaviour and chooses to step away and do the opposite of what they were taught to do by their abusive father. This can be an incredibly difficult pattern to break and requires conscious effort. But making an active choice to not repeat your caregivers' mistakes is something you do have power over.

I am reminded now of my experience with my own biological father. I could have ended up just like him. I went down a path for a while that would have led me there. But in the end, I rejected this. More accurately, I *chose* to reject this, and continue to do so to this day. And with that I reject him, his heinous behaviour and vile opinions – especially about women. My dad thought that dehumanising women made him stronger – it just made him weak and pathetic.

I'm glad my mum chose better too, and that she has a man in her life now that I am happy to call Dad. And I'm glad I've since been able to surround myself with good men – my step-dad, my rugby coaches – who took this very obviously traumatised boy under their wing and planted the seeds of what real masculinity looks like. They showed me what it actually means to be strong, and protective and supporting. They showed me that knowing who you are and being confident in that person, understanding your emotions and being in control are your greatest strengths.

They laid the foundations for my pillar of emotional intelligence, and my mental resilience. Thank you all, great men.

How to develop your emotional intelligence using MIND

I've already covered the FOCUS method above, which is a great tool for building your pillar of emotional intelligence. Now, here is how you use the MIND method to make that pillar even stronger.

Measured success

This may seem like a tricky one to accurately measure, but it's really quite simple. Measuring success with regards to your emotional intelligence means being able to reflect and see a journey of personal progression in your life. It's the ability to look at where you are now compared to where you once were.

Have you ever scrolled through your Facebook/Instagram timeline and cringed at some of the stuff you posted years ago? Are there things that you've done that keep you up at night? Do you have memories that pop up out of nowhere, of a moment where you displayed crappy behaviour towards others, and does this make you feel mortified? Good!

I know it can be embarrassing and confronting, remembering some of the awful things we've done and said (and believe me, everyone has done and said bad things). But this cringing feeling of embarrassment, of shame, means that you've grown since you were that person. You are no longer the person who would do such a thing or behave in such a way. You are aware of how your actions affect others, and you are more empathetic and conscientious. You've learned from your mistakes. In summary, you're more emotionally intelligent.

When I look back at the wildness and the emotional irrespon-sibility of my early twenties, I feel this way. It is a stark contrast to who I am now. It's worth acknowledging how far you've come, how much more control you have now, how you've matured. It's something to be proud of.

In a few years' time, perhaps you'll look back on some of the stuff you do now and cringe. That's okay. A human being is a work in progress, and we're not nor will we ever be perfect. What matters is growth, and reflection on that growth. I understand that it's hard to forgive ourselves for some of the things we've done. Self-forgiveness is one of the hardest skills to master. And perhaps if some of the things we've done in the past are particularly bad, it's difficult not to see ourselves as bad people. But remember, truly bad people don't look back at their actions and feel remorseful. They don't reflect, and they don't grow. You feeling bad about stuff from your past means that you are a good person who wants to do better.

Intrinsic motivation

Whatever you do not change, you choose. This means that if you are dissatisfied with your situation, it is your responsibility to make changes. The motivation to become more emotionally intelligent should be driven by your own desire to improve your situation, whether this is your health, your career, your financial situation or your relationships. How you respond to adversity rises and falls with your emotional intelligence. To repeat what I said earlier, people will often repeat cycles of misery, trauma and anguish until the pain of breaking that cycle becomes less than the pain of repeating it. This is where you become aware that you are the person in charge of your destiny and of your well-being. The choices you make are a reflection of this. It can be difficult to make the choice to break the toxic patterns we find ourselves in.

It's hard work unlearning patterns of behaviour that we've been taught and have repeated throughout our lives. But if you don't, it will stop you from building that pillar of emotional intelligence. And what you're saying then, what you're really communicating to yourself then, is that you're fine where you are. Is that the message you want to send yourself?

Now, in the present

Let's loop back to the FOCUS tool. Being able to use this tool in times of difficulty and stress is brilliant. It's a tried, tested and proven technique to help you manage your emotional state. But you can't do this all the time. It will stop you from thinking about where you are in that moment, from being mindful. In addition to FOCUS, apply the metaphor of the unexpected visitor as well, so you can keep a healthy distance from your emotions and not get swept away by them. The visitor is just one metaphor. Some people like to think of their emotions as a river flowing past. You are standing on the bank, observing your emotions flow. You don't get into the river, but you watch it flow, without judgement. The point of both of these methods of thinking is to pull you out of your emotional state and into observer mode in that moment. Rather than saying, 'I am angry', take a step back, linguistically, and say, 'I feel anger'. Rather than saying, 'I'm scared' say, 'I feel fear'. Do you see how that creates a space between you and the emotion?

Dream big

We tend to set ourselves big goals for what we want in life. A big house, a dream career, a swanky car, a loving partner, a big bank balance, killer abs or running a marathon – all things we might want to work towards. But when was the last time you set yourself an emotional goal? As a society, we're so focused on tangible and materialistic goals that exist outside ourselves that we don't pay attention to what we internally want and need. When is the last time you considered how you want to feel in the future? Have you ever said to yourself, 'In five years' time I want to be content and at peace' or, 'Ten years from now I want to have learned how to love myself'? Those feelings, those goals, don't come from material worth or forces outside ourselves that we think will validate our worth. They come from within, they come from cultivating emotional intelligence and compassion. Set those goals for yourself too. *You* have power over this. How do you want to be feeling in the future?

Exercises

Exercise 1: Breath is power

I know the road to hell is paved with breath exercises, but this one really is very good. It's similar to square breathing but not quite the same. I have it on good authority that this is what is taught to children (and quite possibly nervous adults), before going into an MRI (magnetic resonance imaging) machine. It's very calming. Follow this pattern:

- Breathe in for four seconds (fill your lungs to half capacity).
- Hold for one second.
- Breathe in for another four seconds (fill lungs to maximum capacity).
- Hold for four seconds.
- Release breath steadily for four seconds.
- Repeat four times.

Have you just tried it? Did you feel that instant relaxation? Strange isn't it, that a simple breathing exercise starts a wave of release?

Put simply, by breathing like this we activate our parasympathetic nervous system, which governs our bodily state of 'rest and digest'. It will literally physically calm you down. It is putting the body in the opposite state to the flight/fight/freeze response. That coldness in your stomach, the adrenaline, the cortisol, the tension, the preparation for conflict, it all fades. And, your mind is no longer focused on what's causing you stress, instead it's focused on counting. It's gaining control of your system so you can put yourself in a calmer, more rational headspace, with the prefrontal cortex back in the driving seat to make the correct decision in that moment. So, when you're angry, breathe. When you're scared, breathe. When you're stressing out, breathe. Trust the functions of your body to put you back in a calmer headspace. Learning to control this is learning how to take your power back.

Exercise 2: Listen to your body and relax

Once you've mastered this first exercise, try moving on to this. This exercise will help you hear your subconscious, which will lead to a better understanding of the self, which of course leads to being more emotionally resilient.

The ability to listen to your body is a forgotten art, and that really is a terrible shame, especially as we do actually have the capability to listen to our body with great intent. In order to do this, we must learn to quiet our minds. This is a challenge of course in our day and age of over-stimulation, with our phones ringing, notifications popping up, group chats pinging away, the endless rolling news, and so on. This life is a lot to manage, that's for sure. My mind is regularly overwhelmed with information, and I find myself spending so much of my cognitive energy on all of these stimulating and distracting things that I simply do not have the attention to quietly tune in and listen to my body

to find out what is going on. I'm sure you feel the same, so here's
what you do:

- Remove all stimulants. Turn your phone off, close the
  doors, or even better, get outside to a peaceful place,
  perhaps somewhere green, because we're escaping this
  dystopian nightmare and we going to reconnect with ourselves. One you have escaped and found a peaceful place,
  sit still. We are now going to practise two key components
  of being able to listen to our subconscious, that is, to clear
  the prefrontal cortex and calm the body.
- Now sit in an upright position, not crossed legged in a
  lotus position, nor bolt upright, just a comfortable upright
  position. I like to have my hands in my lap, but they could
  be by your side, it doesn't matter.
- Now, breathe in for 7 seconds, and breathe out for 11 seconds. Fill your lungs and belly up with air and then release
  that air in a controlled and patient way. This is calming
  your body and mind. While your conscious mind focuses
  on your breath, your parasympathetic nervous system is
  activated, and the body will start to relax.
- You're now going to progressively relax yourself. Pick a
  point at the very top of your head, and keep breathing as
  described above. Now imagine a light at this point on the
  top of your head. Where the light is, your body will start to
  relax. Now start moving the light down your body. Move
  it down from the crown of your head to your forehead,
  feeling the muscles there relax. Then move it down to your
  eyebrows, your eyes and eyelids. Imagine the stress leaving
  them. Your ears and ear lobes are next, followed by your top
  lip, your mouth, cheeks and jaw. Your mouth might even
  open slightly from the release of tension. The light moves
  down to your neck and throat, then to your shoulders. It

will move down your left arm first, your biceps and triceps, your left elbow and forearm and wrist, all the way to the ends of your fingers. The same process now happens to your right arm, all the way to your fingertips. Now the light and relaxing feeling move down your body – your lungs and heart, your diaphragm, your stomach, lower back, all the way to your genitals and glutes. The light moves to your hips, followed by your left leg, through to your quad, hamstring, knee, calf, ankle and foot, to the tip of your toes. Repeat that entire process down your right leg until you reach your toes.

Open your eyes. Do you feel more relaxed now?

By focusing on nothing but your breath, and the imaginary light relaxing your muscles, you shift your awareness to your body and how it feels. Now stay in tune with that peace and silence and sit there for a little while longer, breathing calmly.

The more often you practise this the better you'll become at it. This really is a meditative practice that connects your conscious with your subconscious.

Studies have shown that repetition of the process in this exercise allows your prefrontal cortex to increase its connectivity to the amygdala, which means you are hearing your subconscious more clearly. This is a total win, because in a world of overwhelm it's difficult to listen to your body over the racket of modern life. The more you do this, the more you can hear yourself.

Exercise 3: Journalling

Those who over-think should over-write. Journalling is making a comeback, as it should, because it's really helpful to a resilient mindset. So many of us kept diaries growing up, but somehow fell out of the practice of journalling regularly. It's an incredibly powerful tool however, and here's why. Putting pen to paper allows you to give your emotions a voice. Sitting with your conundrums, reflecting on them and writing how you feel about them allows you to create cognitive space to consider and reach more logical conclusions to the struggles that you face.

This works best if it's something that you do regularly. Sitting every night before bed and taking some time to write about your day is an extremely good way to increase your self-awareness, which helps you to regulate your emotions and prevents you from being swallowed by them. Even if you feel completely overwhelmed by the twists and turns of your daily life and the stress this generates, writing down your fears and reflecting on them allows you to see that they're often actually quite manageable, which will have a calming effect on your mood.

Don't forget to also take time to reflect on previous journal entries. Consider your journal to be your owner's emotional manual. When you reflect on what you've written and look back on how you handled your feelings before, you'll understand what your emotional responses are, what events or environments trigger them, what makes you feel uncomfortable and what you can do to manage these situations. Further on, you'll start to see patterns that will help you understand how you emotionally work and why you work that way as a result of the experiences in your life that have shaped you. All of this will help you manage your emotions.

Here are some prompts that can work as a great starting point for your journalling:

1. What wins did I have today? How do I feel about those wins?
2. How did my attitudes, behaviours or beliefs turn a negative situation into a positive one?
3. What are three things that I'm grateful for today?

4. What were my low points today? How did I feel, and why did my subconscious choose that emotion for me?

5. How can I improve tomorrow? What can I do better tomorrow than I did today?

Your answers needn't be an essay, they could even be just a sentence. It's irrelevant how much you write, what's important is that you write for you, not for the clock or to reach a word count. Just write, and do it regularly. Soon, with consistent effort, you'll see the emotional overwhelm flow away from you.

Summary

Emotional intelligence is a complicated process. It feels different for each of us, and it can provide the freedom that we desire to learn, grow and develop. It's our path to becoming resilient and powerful, and, most importantly, to knowing ourselves, our emotions and our reactions. It helps us manage our lives and the outcomes of our actions. Use the processes and techniques discussed in this chapter to develop your understanding of yourself, to really know who you are and why your subconscious chooses the responses that it does. This is not a process that you will master overnight, and, like all growth, it is not linear. The more you do it doesn't necessarily mean that you will get better at it at an equal rate. There will be challenging days and there will be better days, there will be moments of self-control and moments of volatility. The most important part of this process is the willingness to try.

CHAPTER THREE

Physical Health

What you can expect to learn in this chapter:

- How exercise helps develop our mental resilience.
- Why you must take care of your body and how even small things can make a difference.
- What happens to the brain when we exercise and when we don't.
- Four things we can all do to motivate ourselves.

My legs are the heaviest they have ever been. I have lost several toenails, and most of the skin on the bottom of my feet is blistered, sore and has come loose. Even though the rugby boots that I am wearing are blades and not studs, it feels as if they have come through the soles of my boots and are waiting to punch through my foot. I can feel my heartbeat in my knees and hips, and it seems as if the joints have run out of all lubricant – just dry bone grinding against dry bone. The once tight-fitting rugby jersey has now become slightly baggy, my muscles completely drained of any glucose or nutrients, just saggy exhausted bags of tissue under my skin.

I'm not out of breath, but it feels as if I can't breathe deeply enough. I am fairly sure I have drifted off into some form of sleep while moving a few times now. I don't have hunger pains anymore; they have subsided into a numbness. I no longer have conscious thoughts, just abstract emotional reactions that fuel unconscious responses. I am 21 hours into a 24.5-hour Guinness World Record attempt for the longest game of rugby 7s ever played. The match is Horus 7s (the team I am honoured to be a part of) versus Barbarians 7s (a mixture of willing volunteers and a few 'voluntolds'), two teams of equally foolish friends going through an extremely tough event together.

We play full contact rugby for 24.5 hours straight. (We've actually done it twice: the first time was rugby 7s, where each side has seven people on a full-sized rugby pitch with five substitutions – rolling subs – and the second time was rugby 10s.) Full contact means there are broken fingers, bangs to the head, twisted ankles, loss of toenails, blistered feet and tears all round. There are strops and mood swings, there is the deployment of tape, distribution of paracetamol, the release of ibuprofen, the consumption of energy drinks on a level that my liver takes a while to recover from, and the heartbreak whenever anyone asks, 'How much more time left, ref?'

What I realise at this time is the importance of being fully involved, of changing my focus. Just to commit, to be a support runner (someone waiting to catch the ball and take the next hit), to get involved in a ruck no matter how long it goes on. Just put your head down, get your hands on the ball, do not stand out on the wing, no matter how cold and broken you are, hoping but also secretly not hoping that the ball gets passed to you. Get into it. There's nothing better for taking your mind off the suffering and freeze and how miserable you are than fully committing to the experience, even if that experience is painful. Because the moment I stop focusing on the blisters, the rolled ankle, the fatigue and the cold and wet, is when time starts to fly. And at that exact point, the sun breaks out.

When we finish the match, utterly exhausted but chuffed to bits with what we have accomplished, we are sprayed down with champagne, we laugh together, cheer and briefly revel in our success. It is a truly wonderful feeling.

*

I was very physically fit when I played this Guinness World Record-breaking match, which made it a lot easier for me to succeed, and it is worth noting here that other participants who were less fit and not accustomed to pushing their body to the very edges of its physiological capabilities suffered far more than I did. There's a big lesson in this for everyone, no matter what your level of fitness is. Taking care of your body means having to rely far less on the cognitive processes of mental resilience to get you through a challenging event. Good health and physical well-being simply are a huge support when you're facing physical adversity.

When I did my military courses, courses for promotion, for development of skills or to prepare for deployment, I was told that there would be a fitness assessment and that there would be 'arduous events' during these courses. Usually, this would be an assault course, a log and stretcher race, maybe even a tactical insertion into the final phase of the course, which involves moving through often boggy and undulating terrain, carrying full equipment, a heavy rucksack and lots of ammunition. It wasn't until I started doing these courses that I realised that being fit relieved me of a lot of the stress that comes with participating in these kinds of events. I didn't need to worry about the 'arduous' element of the course, because I knew for a fact that I would be in the top third at the very least. It was just one less thing to have to worry about, and having faith in myself really gave my mental resilience a boost.

Through hours of hard work and training, through nutritional discipline and consistent effort to look after myself, I now know that when something is being asked of me that will physically challenge me, I have the capabilities to get the job done. This success is in no small way facilitated by a mindset of accomplishment and the will to challenge myself, which I have developed over decades of competition in professional sport.

I hate the phrase, 'It is what it is'. With an 'it is what it is' mindset, I wouldn't be where I am now. I've gone through childhood abuse, poverty, homelessness, military training and tours. I've picked myself up from the bottom and fought my way up. If I'd had that mindset, I would have stayed where I was, helpless in the situation that I happened to be in when I was younger, a victim to the elements and to my suffering.

In recent years, stoicism has become a more popular and mainstream way of approaching mental resilience, and it is something I subscribe to. Stoicism teaches us a dichotomy of control, that there are two things that you can control: your attitude and your efforts. So instead of standing there, helplessly saying, 'It is what it is', tell yourself, 'It is what I choose to make it'. This attitude, paired with my physical capability, made me nearly unbeatable and gave me a true feeling of achievement at the end of it, despite all the pain I had to endure to get there.

The rugby match wasn't the first time physical fitness had seen me through adversity. From basic training and the infamous P Company (the well-known and extremely challenging military course designed to test a candidate's physical and mental capabilities to serve in the British Airborne Forces), to leadership courses and competitive sport, being physically fit and strong has removed so much worry from my life. As previously mentioned, when it comes to accomplishing my goals, I see it as one less stressor, which helps me not worry about being stuck at the back or failing what I'm set out to do. To be clear, you needn't be at top fitness level to adopt this mindset. I've given you quite extreme examples, but they contain a truth for everyone: if you are taking care of your health, then your risk of debilitating illness shrinks considerably, you will feel better, will have more stamina and will feel good about properly looking after yourself. Your ability to be resilient really is empowered by your physical health.

This isn't the only reason why being physically fit is so important for your mental resilience though. It's also because it is an indicator of certain characteristics that lead to mental resilience.

People who exercise regularly, drink enough fluids, take care of their nutrition and sleep well are more likely to be disciplined, or at least understand the value of a consistent routine. Let's look at what being physically active does for our mental resilience.

Healthy body, healthy mind

Physical fitness and exercise have measurable neurological effects. By flooding the brain with blood and oxygen through exercise, we are better able to create and strengthen neural pathways. We can increase our brain's ability to adapt to change by getting the blood flowing there better and more often. In turn, the ability to adapt is essential to stress management as it allows us to adjust our behaviours to the environment.

One of the things that triggers stress is when we feel we're starting to lose control of a situation. I have found this to be one of the most inspiring and beautiful things about physical fitness in all its forms, from road running, biking, crossfit, boxing, rugby, powerlifting, body-building, strongman, whatever it might be. During those activities, you are taking control of yourself. It also gives you a place in your life where you can escape from the daily stresses of the real world you live in and provides a brief window where you can control the outcome.

I started lifting weights when I was 15. I went to a tiny old chapel that had been converted into a body-building space. It had rusty kit, broken machines and one very angry dog. There were centre-folds from all the classic British dirty magazines plastered across the walls and deafening black metal played there at all hours. This was my safe space. It was where I could go and get away from the pain I was going through as a child. Here, I could shift my focus away from how much I hated school, how confused I was about my relationship with my biological father who had put me and my family through so much grief, from the abuse I suffered at home from him. I felt in my heart that I should love him and that he loved me, but people who love you wouldn't do those things to you, would they?

Once I had discovered that chapel, I stopped wanting to cry every day. I realised then how important this place was to developing a sense of peace and control in my life. It became massive to me. It helped me maintain my sense of self.

How we define 'losing control' is highly subjective. One of the greatest lessons of life is to truly understand, and remember at all times, that the one thing you can always control is how you choose to react. This ties directly into the brilliant teaching of many great people, from Epictetus the Greek Stoic philosopher, to the incredible writings of Viktor Frankl and his experiences in Auschwitz. Those who grasp and practise this are the people who have the steadiest pillars of resilience. Those who understand their own levels of control are also the people who can identify which of their pillars needs the most attention. Therefore, regular physical exercise means enhancing the thought patterns that enable us to build our strength and adaptability of mind, and through this improve our ability to deal with and regain control in stressful situations.

That's not the end of the list of the benefits of exercise on the brain. We can't forget the huge release of dopamine and endorphins. Dopamine is an important neurotransmitter that functions as our reward hormone. It gives us a biochemical 'pat on the back' and it kicks in after eating, sex, and indeed, exercise.

Now imagine that you are struggling hideously in your current life situation. Perhaps your studies are becoming too much, your job is overwhelming or your relationship is going down the pan. It's all getting too much, and you desperately need to find something positive to grab on to. You need to inject a reward into your brain. So, you dig deep and find that one ounce of motivation you still have and pull on your trainers. You go for a run, lift weights at the gym, swim a few laps or go for a bike ride, and your body immediately rewards you for it. For a while afterwards you feel successful, as if you've accomplished something, and your self-worth inflates a little. The next day you challenge your problems a little more head-on, you see things a little more clearly, get stuff done a little quicker, and this in turn relieves some of the pressure inside your head. And guess what – this causes you to get another dopamine reward.

I hope you're starting to see the pattern I'm trying to sketch out for you. These dopamine rewards can become a chain when they're aligned correctly, and in order to get this to work you need to be disciplined. You need to train and exercise regularly, challenge yourself physically regularly to establish this chain. This might look different for everyone. Perhaps you're already a long-distance runner (in which case, good for you!) or a regular weight-lifter, and your challenge here is to keep up the discipline and push yourself beyond what you've already achieved. Perhaps you're not so fit just yet, and instead you take a regular walk at lunchtime, and every time you go a bit further (also, good for you!). Perhaps you like yoga and find a spare 30 minutes in your day to further your practice. Whatever you do, whatever your level of fitness is, the key here is *discipline*. Exercise at regular intervals and pat yourself on the back when you've done it. If you do this, the dopamine response can link up day after day, and this then aids us in taking that first step, then that next step, and then that extra step, and soon you'll be marching towards your goals.

Our brains crave dopamine. It is designed to increase the behaviours that ensure survival of the tribe, which is why it's triggered by food, sex, exercise and achievement. The brain would like as much of this hormone as possible, which leads me to the darker side of this biochemical process. Dopamine is also triggered by the use of alcohol, gambling and certain drugs. And because our brains constantly want more kicks, want another rush of this chemical, the pursuit of dopamine hits can lead us to some very dangerous behaviours and even addiction if we're not in control of it. It's really not so much the act of gambling, or using alcohol, taking drugs, having sex, it is the rush of dopamine that we get from those things that creates the craving after the rush is over. Dopamine really is a drug and must be administered carefully. You must learn to earn it, and to deal with the repetition of its passing.

In the past, I used to indulge in excessive drinking during tough periods of my life. I have now stopped drinking alcohol altogether. The imbalance of hormones from hangovers which made me feel anxious and depressed, the extremities of behaviours while drunk, the embarrassments and apologetic phone calls the next day became the opposite of who and what I was trying to be. It contradicted the identity I was trying to forge for myself of a mental resilience coach. It wasn't who I wanted to be, so I stopped. In four years, I have had perhaps two glasses of red wine and a cheeky sip of Guinness. I *could* drink if I wanted to, but I choose not to. I just don't want to put myself in that position anymore. The clarity of thought I have now, the regulation of my hormones and the time and ability I've gained to enjoy things like food with friends and reading books, instead of wasting days being hungover and remorseful, have improved my life and my mental health dramatically.

To be clear, I'm not at all saying that you need to live your life the way I do. It is your choice what you put in your body, whether it's alcohol, drugs or bad nutrition, and it is your choice to suffer the consequences. However, if you recognise something in my story, and if deep down you know that this is a problem for you too, I would reconsider your habits. You will much feel better for it in the long run, trust me. Instead, you can engage your intrinsic desire to feel good by exercising. Being out of breath and sweaty, striving and struggling will make the dopamine flow in a healthy way. And when you focus on the power of dopamine, and realise you're now in control of it, you'll really start enjoying it.

Next up is another neurotransmitter: endorphins. They are the brain's 'feel-good' hormones. Their effects are similar to those of morphine, and so they can reduce pain and induce a feeling of euphoria. You might have heard the term 'runner's high' and you might have even experienced it when going on a long run or other type of prolonged physical exercise. The endorphins released put you in a relaxed and calm state of mind and can help you push yourself even further.

If we relate this back to when we were cave people, that feeling of euphoria comes from sprinting after your prey, catching your dinner, and securing your immediate future. Endorphins help you cope with stress and can boost dopamine production. The dopamine you receive will then encourage you to repeat what you've done, and so this helps you survive and thrive.

Obviously, we don't live in caves anymore. In the modern world, where a lot of us instead sit in an office all day to secure our supper, we need to create these endorphin-releasing environments for ourselves. We must recreate these physiological responses within our brains to remain healthy.

We still have the same body we did in the Stone Age tens of thousands of years ago, and it hasn't actually evolved to adapt to the sedentary lifestyle most of us live now. This really isn't very healthy for us. We all require an element of struggle and reward, the fight, the success and the euphoria. This falls within our basic psychological needs, and without it we would have been eaten up and driven to extinction a very long time ago.

Thankfully, the process of turning distress into eustress (a healthy, stimulating, positive kind of stress) to improve our lives and mental well-being is not a difficult one, it just takes practice. We know that neural pathways become stronger and more efficient with usage and reinforcement, but weaker and inefficient under a lack of use. With practice, we can acknowledge our stress response and choose to respond in a better way. With insight and reflection, we can come to understand the source of that stress and then use the energy generated by the stress to help us succeed. Making the right decisions, recognising and guiding our stress is not easy, but we make it easier through successful reinforcement of the right neural pathways. It's the repetition and exposure to competition, in this case physical exercise, that will make you better skilled at handling that pressure.

This was covered in great detail in the Emotional Intelligence chapter, but cultivating this starts with being able to listen effectively to your body's physiological responses and understanding what your body is trying to tell you. You need to listen to intuition clearly and learn what will soothe it effectively. Learning about your body, its fears and responses to the world and its challenges, is hard. It becomes much easier, though, when you learn to regularly challenge your body, test its limits, listen when you do so to it begging for you to stop, and for you manage that fear and the resistance it gives to instead say 'just another step'. That is where resilience starts.

There's another piece in the puzzle of how physical health helps us build mental resilience. Without physical exercise, the hippocampus can fall into a state of weakened atrophy. Excessive amounts of stress supress the BDNF (brain-derived neurotrophic factor), the hormone required for brain growth and development.[2] Without this hormone, departments of our brain fall into weakened states. The hippocampus is our emotional memory, and is a close personal friend of the amygdala, our emotional generator. If the hippocampus becomes weaker, it is less able to regulate our emotions. Exercise is an extremely effective way of producing the BDNF required to reverse this process. With regular cardiovascular exercise, this essential part of the brain becomes stronger and more efficient in its tasks regarding emotional memory and assisting with emotional regulation. Ideal.

Taking care of your physical health has many more benefits. It reduces the stress hormone cortisol. It positively affects your relationships too. A study by Devon J. Hensel and colleagues showed the link between physical and mental health disorders and sexual dysfunction.[3] Looking after your physical health dramatically improves the frequency and intensity of your sex life. Feeling fitter and healthier allows you to have more fun with your friends, allows you to play longer with kids and opens up a whole range of other activities for you to enjoy. Imagine next time you're on holiday and wanting to climb a mountain or go for a challenging hike, you can actually enjoy the experience and the scenery rather than being in pain!

Physical fitness improves your life in countless ways, and yet getting started on your fitness journey can be overwhelming and complicated. It's difficult not to compare ourselves to people who are fitter than us, and give up. The key to remember here is that everyone's journey is different. Don't compare yourself to others, instead remember where you started this journey and focus only on your improvement. If you're training to run the London Marathon or just hit your personal best on a 10 k run, that's brilliant. If you've never run a day before in your life, and weeks later manage to run 1 k without stopping to catch your breath for the first time, that's equally brilliant. It's all about YOUR journey.

We're not all built the same, all of us have different challenges. Some of us have injuries, disabilities or long-term illnesses. Some of us battle addiction, obesity or horrific mental health conditions. Whatever your challenge is, there is a starting point for you. Just put on your trainers and go.

Four ways to finding motivation

It can be a real struggle to take the first step to improve your physical fitness. Finding the motivation to get up and go is the biggest hurdle people face, so here are four ways to help you.

1. Pair exercise with achievement

It helps to pair exercise with achievement – you can get some wondrous effects. It's easy to fall into a pattern of feeling that there's no point in putting yourself through all that pain. But if you set a clear goal in your mind about what you want to achieve, whether it's weight loss, simply wanting to be stronger and fitter, or helping your body recover after an injury, suddenly waking up at silly o'clock to go for a run, or do yoga, a Zumba class, rugby or any other activity seems a lot more palatable. After all, why would we bother with striving, growing and improving ourselves without something specific to achieve?

When I was a teenager I was on the British Army's infamous P Company course. This is designed to test a recruit's physical and mental suitability to serve in the British Airborne Forces. The point of this course is to physically trash and exhaust you over an extended period of time, because paratroopers have to be physically fit and able to function under pressure and while scared out of their mind. On this course, I faced one of the greatest physical tests I've ever been through: an event known as 'the log'. Essentially, teams of eight recruits must carry a telegraph pole over undulating terrain for three miles. It is absolutely horrific. It didn't help that the other candidates on the course all happened to be shorter than me, and I'm sure to this day that I therefore had to carry a seriously disproportionate amount of the weight.

It was the most awful three miles I've ever had to walk. You get to a certain point of breathlessness whereby you start biting the air in front of you to get anything in your lungs. My left hand (my right was used to drag the log) was gripping my trousers and I was using it to drag my left leg forward because it wouldn't do it on its own. I was in so much pain and so unable to breathe that I couldn't even cry. Sobs and moans were nothing more than gasps of air, jaw swinging wildly, doing everything I could to force the oxygen into my burning lungs, jelly legs hobbling beneath me.

All ideas that I am in any way anything other than a very normal human with very normal emotions would be dashed away if you had been a fly on the wall at this event. But despite the number of times I begged to myself to quit, to give up and to remove myself from this horrific event, to simply let go of the piece of rope attaching me to the log and carrying its weight, I just couldn't. In the brief moments of respite where perhaps I could have removed myself from the event, I somehow didn't. I made the conscious decision that I would rather die than surrender myself to my own lungs.

This event has sent many a person home, broken many spirits and destroyed countless dreams of becoming an airborne soldier. I am still not sure how, but I managed to complete the course, despite a constant feeling of impending death through exertion.

At the end of the log race, there were five logs and 40 recruits. We stood in a line. The sergeant major of P Company looked as if he was ready to bite my nose off. He was a terrifying man who would stand slightly too close and scan your face when you spoke to him, as though your words were irrelevant and what he was actually doing was measuring you up for weaknesses. He always spoke with the authority of someone who had never been out of his depth in any circumstance. I was an 18-year-old boy, and he was a fully grown man. I was scared of him and remain scared of him to this day – even as a 34-year-old man and 105 kg of relatively lean muscle.

He walked in front of us and addressed the group: 'You lot here can all call your dads tonight and say, "Dad! I stayed on the log!"

and he will be proud, and you will be proud that you have stayed on the single hardest event that the British forces have. This will stay with you for your entire career, and nothing that happens will ever be able to top this.'

As a young soldier – or rather, a soaking wet piece of very malleable clay – can you imagine the effect his words had on my self-esteem? Knowing that I had accomplished something that the vast majority of people fail at made me realise that I did have personal strengths and capabilities. As a result of this, my resilience increased, and this had an incredible effect on my mindset throughout my whole career. To get that sentiment from that man in that position was monumental. The fact that I now believed that I had conquered the hardest physical test that I would ever have to face instilled amazing self-efficacy within me.

Later on, when times were tough, I would think, *this is tough, but it isn't as tough as the log*, even when this simply wasn't true to anyone but me. When I was 20 hours into my Guinness World Record attempt with Horus 7s for the longest played game of rugby, I started telling myself that it was not as bad as the log, and given that I'd stayed on that, all I now had to do was smile and breeze through this speedbump. It no doubt helped me through that ordeal.

Once you understand that achieving things inside the gym, on the rugby pitch, in front of goal posts or wearing boxing gloves can correlate with anything else that you want in your life, then you are already well on your way to having a fulfilling existence. Your endurance on the treadmill will translate into you pushing yourself to meet an important deadline at work. Getting through a gruelling hike or uphill bike ride will help you realise you can in fact handle the sleepless nights as a new parent. Successfully mastering a new yoga pose will show you that you can in fact achieve balance when your life feels hectic and out of control. Consistently exercising will make you realise how strong you actually are and that you can handle what life throws at you. You know that work rate equates to success, you know that effort equals results and that consistency reveals character. These are great things to learn, and important lessons for our mental resilience.

2. Believe you have control

Attribution theory also plays a huge role in how we achieve our goals. Attribution theory is a theory about how an individual attributes the events of their life. It originated with a psychologist in the 1950s called Fritz Heider and has evolved since then.[4] Say, for example, someone very strongly believes in the concept of the universe as a guiding force in their lives, and stars to dictate the outcomes of their life, a belief in 'fate' or 'a plan'. This is known as an 'external locus of control': the things that happen, happen *to* the person, not *because* of the person. An individual who attributes the events in their life to themselves, their own attitudes, behaviours and beliefs, has an 'internal locus of control'. Attribution theory is very prevalent in sports psychology. It encourages athletes to understand that the outcome of a competition lies within them, whether that is on the pitch or in the training.

If you attribute a loss to something outside your control, then you are a slave to it, every time. So, if you are a person who believes that things happen *to* them, that you have no control over any of the events in your life or the direction your life takes, that you are a victim to the whims of the world around you, then you are far less likely to succeed. However, if you are a person who believes that you dictate the outcome of the events in your life, that by hook or by crook, you will find the motivation and energy to ensure success, then you are far more likely to be successful in what you want to achieve.

From the start of the 'log' event, I understood that the weather was uncontrollable, and injuries were mostly uncontrollable, but I could still manage my responses to them. I ensured that I regularly changed my socks when it was my break to eat and hydrate. I seized on that and made sure I pulled on some warm kit as soon as possible. This way I managed to stay on top of any negative feelings, and I could easily attribute the successes of the day to my own actions. I could wholly believe it was I who held control of my success, not something or someone else.

3. Stay in the moment

I picked up so many psychological teaching points from the Guinness World Record 7s and 10s challenges and it gave me brilliant demonstrations of the power of breaking down tasks. I made a killer mistake after about 18 hours of play: I asked for the score. It was ridiculous, as our team was well over a thousand points up, and that knowledge absolutely destroyed me. It nearly broke my spirit. Finding this out was so detrimental to me that I had to completely readjust how I approached the whole challenge. I had to do this in order to prevent a catastrophic collapse of motivation.

I decided to get fully engaged in playing and think of nothing else. I even began to recite to myself, 'there is no pain, there is only rugby'. I would focus on who was passing to who, where I should be standing and what I should be doing in that moment alone. In truth, this is mindfulness. I was focusing my mind on the present moment and the steps that I had to take to keep going, which is exactly what I teach my athlete clients to do. I wasn't thinking about the lack of skin on the bottom of my feet, nor the missing toenails, nor the swelling in my hand. My thoughts were purely on the game. After all, this is how a rugby match of 80 minutes should be played, but after 18 hours this becomes harder to manage. By focusing on the game this way, I found that the time did begin to slide away, that things did become better and even enjoyable again. Especially when the supporters – and therefore cake – began to arrive. There was even a magical moment when a C130 aircraft flew over; the back ramp was down and the load master waved out the back to us, all at about 500 ft from the ground.

So, focus your mind on the task at hand, what you're doing in the moment, and not how much more you've got until you're done or the result itself. Focusing my mind in this way and taking note of these moments of enjoyment really helped me to pull through.

4. Use your success as fuel

The log and the rugby match will stay with me forever. I draw on these memories whenever I need to flex my mental resilience muscles, or just to remind my better half of a time when she thought I was cool. These times are a wellspring for self-efficacy. Sure, there were some blasted tough moments, but that final whistle was euphoric, and the taste of the winners' cake was unbelievable. The sun shone, we all laughed, partners dutifully fussed over us, and even the most broken men on the team dared to smile. The challenge has had a lasting positive effect, and has helped multiply my motivation in other, totally unrelated, areas of life. Even now, in the daily slog of life, when I find myself having to do paperwork for my taxes after I've been working all day and I'm exhausted and unmotivated, I can take a moment to appreciate the log race and the rugby match, and these still supercharge my motivation. I use them for self-growth and motivation as a simple visualisation of my success, safely stored in my emotional memory. In a way, this illustrates how 'success breeds success' and why 'winning is a habit': those emotional memories reward and spur you on towards your current goals. So, make sure to draw on every success you have and use that as the fuel to drive you forward and to help you face other challenging situations in your life.

How to take care of your Physical Health pillar using MIND

Looking after your physical health empowers you and fills you with self-efficacy. You can grow and change immensely the more control you have over your physical output. Your confidence will inevitably become higher because of that control, the autonomy you have over your health and how you feel. A lot of people I meet in the gym once upon a time were larger people who have chosen to take control. Some of the women I work with once suffered with eating disorders and body dysmorphia. They are now re-taking control of their physical health and confidence, growing and changing and becoming stronger because of it. Your pillar of confidence also grows with every step in your physical health that you take.

This is how you use the MIND method to develop positive physical health.

Measurable success

It is incredibly important to highlight here how much we need goals. We need to know that we are achieving the things we set out to achieve, that we are growing and developing and learning, and we're empowered to do this ourselves. That is what focusing on your physical health provides. I don't necessarily mean following a body-building programme, or trying to get as enormous as possible, or as fit as possible or running a huge distance or any form of the more extreme versions of physical training. I am simply referring to the importance of being in control and working regularly on your physical health. To focus on it is to provide yourself with purpose and a challenge for you to aspire to. It will dramatically increase your quality of life, and it's a lot easier to be mentally resilient when you aren't struggling to breathe, move, sleep or just live.

This is going to sound unbelievable, but if you want to measure the progress you're making in your physical fitness with regard to your mental resilience, throw out the scales and the measuring tape. Instead, ask yourself: what is it that I actually want to achieve? Usually the answers to this are quite subjective: I want to look better, I want to be fitter, I want to be stronger, and ultimately it all comes down to, I want to feel better about myself. Instead of weighing yourself, take neutral photos of yourself in neutral light; do this consistently every few weeks and track your progress that way. Keep track of how far you go on your runs and pat yourself on the back when you break your personal best. Make notes of how much you lift and once you surpass it, celebrate. Most importantly, keep track of how you feel on this journey. You can do this with a mood diary, and there is an exercise below that will help you with this. Whatever you want to achieve, set yourself goals and always ask yourself along the way how you feel. When we feel better about ourselves through successes, whether small or big, our resilience increases.

Intrinsic motivation

We've discussed in great detail above how to remain motivated on this journey of taking care of your body. Looking towards your achievements, realising you have control and focusing in the moment all help keep up your motivation to stay fit and healthy. What we also need to do is look beyond what keeps us motivated in the moment and towards what will keep us going longer term. You'll remember that as a young soldier, knowing that I was physically fit would feed into how I would approach any challenge as I knew I could handle it, which increased my enjoyment of the task as well as my self-esteem and self-belief. But your life doesn't have to involve assault courses to reap the benefits of being physically fit. A healthy body means a healthy brain, which increases your cognitive fitness as well. More efficient energy usage means you're more energetic and less lethargic, which means greater ability to have more fulfilling days. Think about how much more you'd enjoy that festival, that wedding, that night out dancing, that sunny afternoon chasing your kids in the park if you were fitter. It means that walk through Liverpool Street tube station (or wherever you commute to) becomes that much less taxing. It means climbing a few flights of stairs in your office becomes a piece of cake. And those few flights of stairs can turn into a hike in the forest with a loved one, walking up a hill in a national park to enjoy the view, climbing a mountain on a life-changing holiday, and many other memories you'll cherish forever. A healthy body means a longer life with more diverse experiences and adventures to fill it with. That's ultimately where we pull our motivation from to keep going – improving our quality of life. Take note of the increase of meaningful experiences you have, and use that as fuel to keep going. Look after your body, you only get one.

Now, in the present

It would be easy at this point, to simply shout one of those 'motivational' social media quotes designed to keep you focused on your exercise. Something like 'Pain is weakness leaving the body' or, 'Sweat is just fat crying' or, 'Pain is temporary, pride is forever!'

If you are like me, however, these will make you roll your eyes. They do literally nothing for me. They completely miss the point of what improving your physical health is about, and I find them so cringy that they have the opposite effect on me.

Instead, what I have found to be most effective for keeping my mind in the present moment focused on what needs to be done, even when my body is tired and has had enough, is following a simple two-step process: the 'what' and the 'how' of pain.

The 'what' refers to me reminding myself exactly what pain is. Pain is nothing more than my body trying to tell me how much danger it thinks that I am currently in. Your body, that is intrinsically built to survive, wants you to stop because it wants to feel safe. That screaming in your head to stop is just your body trying to convince you that you are in way more danger than you actually are.

The 'how', is how I overcome this. I have something that I say to myself very often: 'Left foot, right foot, your body will follow'. I repeat that to myself as I am running. I understand that I must keep pushing, even though my body is wired for survival and would happily see me quit and return to homeostasis. It seems like an absolutely ridiculous state of affairs that the same body that begs me to stop exercising is the same body that gets depressed if I don't exercise. Literally a walking contradiction. I use the knowledge that pain is my body's misconception about how much danger it thinks I'm in, alongside the 'left foot, right foot' exercise. It helps me bring my focus into taking the next step, and then another. I repeat this until I'm finished.

Dream big

According to Socrates, 'No man has the right to be an amateur in the matter of physical training. It is a shame for a man to grow old without seeing the beauty and strength of which his body is capable.' The human body is an amazing thing, it really is. I don't mean to sound all romantic and gushy, but it is true. If you place your body in a new environment with different challenges, it will adapt to it. Think about astronauts who have to train in outer space to keep their strength up as the lack of gravity means they start shedding muscle mass. That is an extreme example of the process that I am referring to, but it's true. The evolution of your body depends on the environment in which you choose to place it. This means that you should never underestimate what your body is capable of. If you push yourself and exercise regularly, your body will grow stronger, your cardiovascular system will become more efficient, your heart will become healthier, your bones stronger, and you will both see and feel the effect. Most importantly, your resilience will grow with it. A thousand-mile journey starts with a single step. Just because you can't run 10 k now, it doesn't mean you can't do it at all, it just means that you need to start at a level that works for you and work your way up. If you do, 1 k will turn into 2 k, which will turn into 5 k, and further along the line you will look back and be astonished at what you've achieved. What you put in directly correlates to the results you'll see. So, decide what you want to achieve and aim for that, however unattainable it might feel right now. Whatever you can dream up for yourself, that is what the body can achieve. Exercise should be a celebration of what your body can achieve, not a punishment. Celebrate its brilliance. It's an incredible machine, and it is difficult to manage but it is so worth it when you do it well. Whatever you can dream, dream big, and if you can dream big, dream even bigger.

Exercises

The exercises here are for everyone, regardless of the start point of your health.

Exercise 1: Hydration

From now on, your goal is to drink three litres of water every day. It's a basic thing everyone who is working on their Physical Health pillar should do. Nutrition can be quite subjective to an individual's personal needs, but good hydration is a goal for everyone.

Get yourself a decent water bottle. It needn't be some unnecessarily large one-gallon container to let everyone on the train know how superior your water consumption is. It's just so it's accessible to you when you need it. Most people don't meet their daily recommended water intake – maybe we get busy and forget, or maybe we choose more attractive beverages like coffee and pop instead, but that won't do here, it has to be water.

To encourage me to drink my daily water target (which is a bit higher at five litres), I have a filled water bottle by my bed, and I carry another one with me at all times. I've covered it in stickers from fitness brands and veteran-owned companies, so it's personalised and I have an affinity towards it. It's worth making your bottle personal to you so it becomes important to you.

Now that you have your water and your bottle, set alarms or reminders in your phone to drink the water. When they pop up, don't ignore them because you're busy doing something else, take a break and drink the water. In time and with repetition, you will start remembering to drink water automatically, and it will become a habit, and the need for the reminders will likely fade.

Exercise 2: Keep a mood diary

A very important part of building your pillar of physical health is tracking how you feel while on your journey. The best way to do this is to keep a mood diary. That's right, a mood diary, not a food diary. Track your mood every day, perhaps in a journal, or in an app (there are many great ones free to download) and see how your mood and sense of self improve as you keep up your exercise routine. Make special notes if you want as well, and ask yourself these questions every day then compare your answers to previous entries:

1. How do I feel?
2. How do I feel about my exercise routine and the goals I've set?
3. How do I feel about myself?

In time, you'll see that, overall, your mood will improve. The way you see yourself will shift. And you'll learn some real truths about yourself that you didn't know before. It is often in the darkest places of our fitness journeys, the hardest parts when we just want to quit, that we see aspects of ourselves we didn't see before. In my case of world record attempts, or attached to a log on P Company, or while stumbling down some godforsaken mountain underneath an impossibly heavy barbell, or pushing on to start a 5 a.m. run, that's when I learned who I really am. I found new beliefs and capabilities in those dark places, stripped of my ego and all pretence. It is in these moments that you build your mental resilience.

Exercise 3: Set yourself an achievable goal

Start with setting yourself a reasonable and achievable goal, whatever that might look like to you. I know that everyone faces different challenges when it comes to their physical health, which is why it's so important that you set goals that are manageable for you. The point is that the achievable goal is only the first step towards a bigger goal. One of the most derogatory things I hear people say about themselves is how insignificant their goals feel compared to others around them. This is simply not true. The point is not to do better than someone else, it's to do better than your own previous personal best, even if it's just by a small margin. Every 20 k runner started at 1 k. Every person you see doing a handstand on their yoga YouTube account was once wobbling on one leg about to give up on their practice. You're looking at end results. This is especially important to note for people who have chronic conditions or disabilities. Whatever you're facing, your body deserves to be taken care of, it deserves to be the best it can be, and the only way it will become that is if you set yourself achievable goals that feel manageable to you. When you achieve them with relative ease, it will bring you fulfilment and spur you on for next time, when you'll go just a little further. Achieving these manageable goals will boost your self-worth and resilience. Start small and work your way up.

Exercise 4: Bubble of success

I have a powerful meditative practice that I learned as a young soldier. I now use it before big performances, endurance events, rugby matches and public speaking. I have found this to be extremely effective for managing the pressures ahead of a performance or when I'm training so I can feel in control and able to push myself. It's called the 'bubble of success' and here's how you do it.

First, find a place where you can do this exercise for a few minutes undisturbed. Once you've found that peaceful spot, stand completely still and close your eyes. Now focus on your breath. Take deep, strong breaths and breathe out completely. As you breathe in, make sure you're 'belly breathing'– that is deep breathing that pushes your diaphragm down, making it feel as if you're filling your belly with air as opposed to your upper lungs. Do this as rhythmically as possible.

You'll now start progressively relaxing your body. Start at the very top of your head and work your way down, releasing tension in your muscles along the way. I like to imagine a beam of light around me, moving down as my body slowly starts to relax. Relax the muscles in your face – eyebrows, eyelids, nose, mouth – move down to your neck and shoulders, down each arm to the fingertips, down your chest, stomach, lower back, bum, thighs, knees, calves and feet, all the way to the end of your toes. Focus on relaxing each part very deliberately and consciously, working your way through your body step by step and feeling the connection to that part of your body as you release the tension they hold. Keep breathing calmly and rhythmically through this process.

Now, imagine a bubble has formed around you. The diameter of this bubble should be your arm span, much like Michelangelo's Vitruvian Man. This bubble is your own, personal space, and within it you are the very best version of yourself. Imagine the bubble as a protective armour that doubts, negative feedback, self-sabotage and lack of self-belief cannot penetrate. The bubble is the space in which you believe in yourself, and it does not allow in anything that will undermine your confidence. In this bubble, you are in control, you have the power and you cannot be defeated by anything. In this bubble, there is only success. You own that space, it's yours and yours alone.

Summary

Taking care of your body and improving your physical fitness will provide you with countless benefits in all aspects of your life. A key facet of this is improved brain function, and with that a better balance of neurochemicals and hormones in your brain. There are also thought patterns and habits that you can successfully reinforce by regular physical exercise, as it teaches you that you are in fact capable and persistent and able to get through the challenges you set for yourself. This will translate to dealing with stressful events in your daily life, as being physically fit and knowing you can push through the pain to achieve a goal means you can do this in all areas of your life. Keeping active will improve your life in so many ways, and it will increase and diversify the meaningful experiences that you will fill your limited time on earth with.

Remember that everyone's journey is different and comparing yourself to others is a fruitless exercise. Only measure your progress based on your own achievements, and feel proud of what you've achieved, even if the gain feels minimal. Every small step takes you one step closer to your bigger goal and should be celebrated. Be proud of your body and what it can achieve. Pick exercise that works for you. Every single human on the planet enjoys different physical experiences. If you start running and find it's not for you, don't throw the baby out with the bath water and give up on exercise altogether – there are countless other ways in which you can keep fit and there is something out there that you will enjoy. Once you find it, you'll see that it will stop feeling like a punishment and will become rewarding instead, which will make it far more likely that you will keep it up.

The fitter and healthier you become, the stronger your mental resilience will grow. You will be practised in overcoming pain and struggle, you'll understand the power of consistency, you'll know you need to work for the things you truly want and will become disciplined as a result. Throughout this process, be kind and patient with yourself. The smallest win is still a win. The losses are lessons.

Lastly, remember this: your mind lives in your body. Make it a good place to be.

CHAPTER FOUR

Goals

What you can expect to learn in this chapter:

- Why traditional goal setting is not effective.
- Why fulfilment and identity are important.
- How to treat our failures.
- How to achieve our goals.

I am sitting next to Rob 'Squeaky' Andrews. For those who grew up watching rugby union in the 1990s, you will understand my excitement – the shortness of breath as I hang on his every word, the clamminess of my hands, the self-consciousness, the internal dialogue about the sweat I all of a sudden notice dripping down my back, how embarrassed I am that I have a curly bit of hair sticking out at the front of my head that makes me look like a Wish version of Superman. It is a warm day in sunny Brighton, and I have been invited to be the guest speaker at Sussex County Cricket Club, which seems incredibly bizarre to me, considering that the person sitting with me is an actual English rugby hero. He had 71 appearances for England, scoring 396 points, he's a fly-half hero and here he is, just chatting to me.

We're discussing motivating young cricketers, and how strange it seems to him that he needs to motivate anyone to play at an elite level of a sport. Rob is the chief executive at Sussex County Cricket Club, and he and his team invite small business owners in once a month and allow a guest speaker to come and talk. My talk was about

*emotional resilience and managing pressure, and I think it went well
and seemed to resonate with my audience. Rob is explaining to me
why he finds it so weird that the young cricketers must have goals to
set for themselves, that they must train and work and be motivated
constantly to get results, which requires extrinsic motivation, a process
that Rob finds confusing. This man, who played at such a high level
in Rugby Union, was bemused by the idea that these young sportsmen
would not have the same sense of enthusiasm for their sport that he
did, every day being a celebration of mud and bruises and camaraderie
with his fellow rugby enthusiasts (heavyweights such as Will Carling,
Jeremy Guscott, Martin Johnson and Lawrence Dalaglio come to mind
here). This leads to a very stimulating conversation with the legend
that I grew up idolising, watching those incredible England games,
the players covered in mud and blood and wearing heavy cotton rugby
shirts – a very different game to what we now see.*

*I enquire into Rob's childhood. To have reached such an incredible
level of professional rugby suggests a very deep and intrinsic motivation
to play. It wasn't just that he played the 71 games for England – it's
the hundreds and hundreds of other games, the thousands of passes,
tackles and kicks that are important to note here. Rugby is something
that the man obviously loved, hence why he played so much of it. We
are now deep in conversation, wading through childhood experiences.
He tells me about running around the farm where he grew up with his
brother, playing in the mud, fighting with each other, rolling around
and being called in for food and a bath. You can tell from the way he
speaks that these are very fond memories.*

*This reveals the very source of his intrinsic motivation: in playing
rugby professionally as an adult, he was recreating these much-loved
events of his childhood. He was satisfying the needs of his inner child. He
was so in love with what he did that he needed no extrinsic motivation,
no outside nudges or pushes or nods to achieve it. He simply loved it.*

*It would of course, be extremely naive of me to discount that there
were difficult days, tough games and injuries that would cause much*

emotional distress. That's part of any competitive sport, especially one where the injury rate is so high. I describe my theory to him, and he seems to have a moment of realisation. He seems to understand that the legends of English rugby that he played with were recreations of his childhood relationship with his brother. This is why he enjoyed the game so much and why it feels so strange to him that the younger players need external motivation – he simply did not need it himself.

I am using this introduction to highlight a very valid point about goal setting. If we were to take a closer look at goals you have set for yourself versus the goals that you have actually achieved, it would likely show that traditional goal setting is actually a really terrible way of doing business. It rarely pays off, and there are some very good reasons for this. Most important of all, staying motivated to achieve your goals is much tougher than you think. Even when we set a goal and break it down into specific, measurable, achievable and relevant steps, having to do a major overhaul of this plan when one of these steps is no longer achievable is a really exhausting process that, for the amount of squeeze, yields very little juice. The more goals we set that we don't live up to, the more our belief in ourselves gets eroded, which in turn affects our mental resilience.

How we set goals and why it doesn't work

The reason why setting goals is so important to a resilient mindset is because direction brings achievements, which in turn brings motivation. Achieving something makes us feel good, and we are far more likely to repeat a behaviour if it makes us feel good. This leads us to become resilient and motivated to achieve and strive because we know that there is a reward for our hard work, and that we will feel satisfied and highly likely to repeat the successful behaviour. But there are things that could get in the way.

External factors

The traditional method of goal setting – which you might be familiar with as SMART goals – is something that the military attempts time and time again but rarely with any real success. Soldiers are expected to set themselves goals every year, which they have to achieve in time for their next yearly review. But of course, they themselves have no actual say over their career trajectory, much as they have no control over global politics, pandemics, natural disasters, injuries, welfare or, indeed, life itself, all of which can and do have influence on a military career.

So, what everyone does instead is update their goals to things that they have actually achieved in hindsight, the day before their yearly review. Most people can probably relate to this. If you work in an office job, for instance, you might be familiar with the feeling of setting targets and a year later realising you haven't achieved half of them. You may have had a list of brilliant ideas and directions, and planned out a year of excellent career progression, but reflecting a year later you realise that you're no closer to that promotion than you were six months ago.

What has happened here? More often than not, external factors get in the way. Maybe the time allocated to you for a project wasn't enough and you haven't managed to finish it just yet. Another project you assumed would happen this year has been moved to next year because of budgeting issues. Perhaps the week when you were supposed to do that big presentation you were struck with a horrible stomach bug. Perhaps your kids have had issues at school and your focus, rightly, was on them and their welfare, so you had to move some deadlines on.

Does this sound familiar? The thing to focus on here, though, is expectation versus outcome, and the lack of flexibility we grant ourselves in this process. Sometimes you may not meet a goal because you underperformed. But often, it's due to an external circumstance which is outside our control, yet we blame ourselves for the negative outcome anyway. This in turn affects our self-esteem and, in the long run, our mental resilience.

A great way to look at this idea of external factors influencing our goals is to think of it as like the weather. Have you ever booked a trip abroad and had sky-high expectations that were not met? Say you've booked a brilliant beach holiday at a luxury resort but when you get there, it is pissing down with rain for the entire holiday. Of course, this is really disappointing and I'm not saying that you don't have a right to be upset. But was there anything you could have done about this? No! This all came down to the weather, which is totally outside your control. Being hard on yourself about this would be completely counterproductive. So why blame yourself for things you can't control while trying to achieve your goals?

Motivation comes from within

If you are breaking down each step towards your goal meticulously, whether that's writing your goals down in a special notebook, pinning them to a vision board or having them in an app with reminders and notifications of what you need to do each day, in my exhaustive experience you are going to struggle with goal setting this way because, quite simply, you must remain motivated at all times. Every single day you will have to push yourself and put in effort to force yourself to do the things you set out to do, to make the behaviour that leads to the goal happening. Usually this involves the denial of pleasurable activities – 'You can take a break once you've completed this', 'You can't have lunch until you finish this task', 'You can't go to football practice/dinner with your friend/cinema with your partner until you've ticked off these tasks', and so on. And how long are you expected to maintain that motivation for? Forever, until the end of time? Doesn't that sound completely exhausting?

Consider this example: if your goal is weight loss – a very common goal – we often say to ourselves that we are going to deny ourselves the foods that have caused the issue in the first place, most likely junk food, for the rest of our lives. So what happens when you reach your goal weight? Will you wobble and reintroduce the foods you cut out and possibly gain the weight back? Be honest, can you really deny yourself chocolate for the rest of your life? (Short answer: no, you can't, it's too fantastic, especially popping candy chocolate.)

With this denial mindset, you will inevitably slip back into old habits and quite possibly gain that weight again, only to leave you right back where you started, devastated, angry, demotivated, exhausted and disappointed in yourself. You'll likely blame your perceived failure on your self-efficacy, and along the way damage other future goal setting. This is when we start to think things like, 'I always fail', 'I can't do this anyway so why even try', 'I am useless', and so on. And this fear of failure, and fear of the confirmation that we are somehow incompetent, is the reason why a lot of people simply don't even start at all, believing that their inability to achieve a goal is in some way down to them being unfixable and broken. You can see how this in turn affects our resilience.

Some people even set unachievable goals, knowing that they will not achieve them, just to reinforce their belief that they are useless, a belief usually handed to them by their primary caregivers and unfairly manifesting in their adult life. I have seen people self-sabotage goals and relationships simply so that they can say, 'I told you so' or, 'I knew this would happen' to the person who had the audacity to believe in them and challenge them to be their best. They seek to further and affirm that feeling of unhappiness and establish that their version of being right is more important than finding fulfilment.

This is simply pride, and pride will rust your mental resilience. Let me be clear: to be good at something, you must first be bad at it. In order to learn, you first have to be wrong. You have preconceptions and understandings of a process or task that are flawed, and your inability to admit these very human things will have a derogatory effect on you achieving success. You likely won't want to achieve it anyway because it inevitably involves failure, and it is safer to not challenge yourself, to not set that goal, especially when this state is self-inflicted by pride and the fear that others will perceive you as negatively as you perceive yourself (spoiler: they do not). This will prevent you from ever developing resilience. You have to fail to be successful. As the renowned physicist Niels Bohr once said, 'An expert is a person who has made all the mistakes that can be made in very narrow field.'

Take language learning for example. No one wakes up one day and suddenly knows how to speak French. The way you learn to speak French, aside from cramming vocabulary and grammar, is to speak it badly. For every mistake you make, there will be a correction (whether from a teacher, yourself, or a French person at a patisserie in Paris who refuses to serve you until you pronounce 'pain' correctly), and these corrections continue until you get it right. The only way to learn a language is to fail constantly, be corrected constantly, until you get it right and it becomes second nature. That makes sense, doesn't it? So why not apply this to the other goals in your life? Why be afraid of failure and be discouraged if you don't first achieve your goal?

Also, and this really is the key, consider why you wanted to learn French to begin with. There has to be an internal reason why you're pushing yourself through this, as humiliating as it can feel to be making mistakes constantly, to be failing constantly on your way to success. Was it that you wanted to read French books in their original language? Do you want to get closer to a friend or partner whose native language is French? Have you always wanted to buy a house in the French countryside and live out your days there? These are all very real, deeply personal reasons to want to do something, to push ourselves to that next step. We need this intrinsic motivation to keep going. So, think about your goal. Why do you want to achieve it? What's the deep-seated reason you've set yourself this goal? When you figure that out, the failing and picking yourself up along the way will become a piece of cake.

In the end, intrinsic motivation comes down to fulfilment. That's what Rob Andrew found on the boggy pitches of the 90s. He found fulfilment in the mud, reminding him of his childhood and the experiences that brought him such joy when he was small, so his journey to becoming an England legend was very much influenced by this, because it was such a solid part of his identity. He played in the mud as a child and he loved it, so he did it as an adult. It was him and it became him.

Forging a new identity

This brings us to the next point of goal setting: forging a new identity related to your goals. This is such an incredibly powerful thing to do, and it almost guarantees success. In fact, a study by Eline Meijer and colleagues, published in 2018, has shown that alcoholics are far less likely to touch an alcoholic drink ever again if they refer to themselves as 'teetotal' when offered a drink, rather than 'trying to quit'.[1] One of these implies a strong identity change, the other to having to remain motivated throughout. Your identity and how you perceive yourself is so important because it makes developing behaviours that reinforce that identity so much easier, and this is a critical factor in finding fulfilment in your goals. Allow me to elaborate: take the definition of 'veteran' as listed by the Ministry of Defence: 'anyone who has served for at least one day in Her Majesty's Armed Forces (Regular or Reserve)'.

It is important for us first to understand what this word really means so we can see how a person who identifies themselves as such sees themselves. You would be amazed how hard I have to work with so many of my clients to get them to step away from this word. I call it the 'V' word. I really can't stand it, and here's why.

Many people leave the Army with hopes and dreams for their future, and beliefs about themselves and what they can achieve. No matter how long ago their service was, they wear their regimental T-shirts and quite possibly grow enormous beards, buy a motorbike and sew lots of cool patches about skulls and death on their jackets. Despite them no longer being in the armed forces, a lot of them never ever manage to change their identity. They remain a veteran until the day they die, and even then, their funeral will likely be completely military themed, short of ceremonial gun salute. It's fine of course to see yourself a certain way, but clinging to an identity this desperately can (and in this example often will) hold back a person's potential to achieve something else with their life. They never truly leave the military, they remain what the Army made them, and therefore they can't become anything else.

This is where I step in and discuss the pros and cons of this approach with them. There are brilliant things they have learned from military service, like discipline, physical fitness and well-being, respect for others and, of course, all forms of courage. They are so conditioned by the risk of punishment that, for example, most will never be late for anything ever again. I was once late to university due to a train strike, and I was panicking that my well-educated and very softly spoken professor would make me do press-ups in a puddle. He didn't of course, but the point still stands – I will not be late to anything if I can help it.

Some of the traits and elements of identity that military service can give a person are extremely powerful. But if you will always be just that soldier, how on earth can you ever expect yourself to grow and become something else? One of the key aspects of a successful transition from military life to civilian life is the ability to find a civilian identity, to find your 'Rob Andrew' style of fulfilment and to pursue that goal with gusto and love. And to do that, you must first discover what it is that you want to become.

The changing of identity is something that the military does very well. On my first day in the Army as a young, extremely spotty 18-year-old with a recently shaved head, wearing a crisp uniform with uncomfortable boots that were securely laced, I stood in front of my section commander. This was a man who would go on to have an extremely successful career. He asked me: 'Name?' I replied, 'Jim, Jimmy, Jimbob, any variation of James really.' He went wild. 'Nobody gives a fuck what your first name is. I mean your last name, you fucking toilet!'

He was right, that version of myself had been left behind. I was now having an identity change. My goal was to become a soldier of the British Army, and to achieve that, I had to let go of huge parts of me. I had to adapt new ways of walking, of talking, of eating. The people around me did the exact same thing. We all became different people.

What was truly fascinating about this, looking back, was that those who attempted to retain a sense of their individuality before the military (mostly because they had come from a childhood that helped them develop a strong sense of self) were far more likely to fail. Those of us who became completely indoctrinated, and dare I say, radicalised, were far more likely to succeed. We were fully immersed, and everything that we did was to push ourselves towards that pass-off parade and the joining of our regiments. It became our identity.

This is just an observation of how the military has two processes to achieve the same outcome. One of those things, changing your identity, is proven and very successful. The other, which we'll refer to as SMART goals, seems to be out of a textbook and very ineffective. As discussed already, this type of goal setting is rigid and unflinching, quite possibly with exact times and dates and a very specific methodology for achieving a goal that allows no space for mistakes, lack of motivation or the inevitability of life getting in the way. If you are going to set a goal, you stand a far greater chance of success if you shift your identity to fit that goal.

To get back to the example of losing weight, rather than using the language 'I am trying to lose weight', instead identify yourself as a self-proclaimed 'gym rat'. This isn't about denying yourself the pleasure of chocolate or sweets or takeaways, it is about changing who you believe you *are*. You drink your water, you do your squats, you eat your fruit and vegetables, you train hard and you focus on your health. The excess weight that you lose is a by-product of your identity change. You now receive pleasure from denying yourself over-consumption of chocolate, sweets and takeaways because that is who you are, you are a fitness freak, you are a 'gym rat'.[2] James Clear writes about this in his book *Atomic Habits*, which is a brilliant resource on habit forming.

Goal setting and the brain

Let us now examine the neuroscience of goal setting because it is incredibly interesting. Essentially, the neurons in our brain tend to form repeating cycles. The brain is a huge energy waster, despite its complexity and brilliance, and it is constantly in energy-saving mode, trying to use as little energy as possible. This means that the more we repeat a behaviour, the less energy it will take from us. This is of course, by design. As cave people, we had no idea how many calories we'd have available to us on any given day, so we evolved a process for reducing the energy expenditure of the brain. This is the process we know as 'forming habits'. That's right: a habit is an action that has been repeated so many times that it requires minimal thought and energy to be completed. In this process, the neurons have been sealed in a very thin layer of fat called the myelin sheath, and this reduces the expenditure required for one neuron to communicate with another.

So, when we repeat an action, it becomes increasingly easier to complete it. Fantastic, right? To bring it back to goals, the best thing you can therefore do to ensure that you will achieve your goals is to actively manipulate this process. In order to generate a new identity for yourself, you have to actively repeat the behaviours that are in line with your desired identity over and over again, until they become second nature.

The very basis of habit changing is having to go against what your brain is telling you to do, to diverge from the habits stored in your neurons. Constantly battling against what's easy for your brain and picking the opposite route can become exhausting, and this is where you tend to run out of motivation. But, if you simply start to identify as a different person entirely and adopt the behaviours in line with that identity, then to *not* follow those behaviours will eventually start generating distress, and it'll become much easier, much faster. Fascinating, right?

This is where your Goals pillar feeds into your mental resilience. It's not enough to simply set goals for ourselves. We must reassess our identity and who we believe we are. We must reflect on this introspectively on a daily basis and decide if who and what we are is getting us closer to our desired destination.

Austrian psychiatrist and Holocaust survivor Viktor Frankl, who you might know from his brilliant book *Man's Search for Meaning*, has written about his experience of being taken to Auschwitz and surviving the worst a person can suffer through.[3] While there, he observed that it wasn't just the horrific experience of the camp that influenced the fate of a person, but also the way they choose to respond to these inhumane circumstances. He argues that even if everything is taken away from you, you still have control over one thing: how you choose to react. And this ultimately comes from within, not from external sources. Frankl is the creator of 'logotherapy', a school within psychotherapy that describes the search for meaning in life as the main motivator for human beings. I highly recommend you pick up his book, it's absolutely incredible.

Frankl also agrees with Nietzsche's saying that 'He who has a why to live for can bear almost any how.' A 'why' always far outweighs any 'how', which is a similar point to the excellent one Simon Sinek makes in *Start With Why*.[4] The strength of identification over conscious action will give you purpose, which will ultimately lead to success and the strengthening of your mental resilience.

I have a great example to illustrate this. One of my favourite people on the planet is body-builder Chloe Pickford. She came to me about two years ago struggling with motivation, anxiety and a lack of purpose. We talked about her already very successful body-building career and how, due to Covid-19 and other related challenges, she had lost her motivation and routine.

To get her back to the top, we defined what it would mean to become an International Federation of Bodybuilding and Fitness (IFBB) professional (a huge deal – becoming a real, certified pro is an incredible feat, and the IFBB is the only real way of doing it). Together, we decided what an IFBB pro eats and drinks, how an IFBB pro meditates and journals, how they interact with others and speak themselves, how they sleep, breathe, eat and take control. Two years later, this wonderful woman was awarded her IFBB pro card. She cried on stage and several more times after that while we celebrated her success. She deserved it. She's calm, controlled, focused and brilliant. But really, she had already won her IFBB pro, they just hadn't given her the card yet. She had already adopted the behaviours that led her to victory. That version of Chloe Pickford, that we call *the* Chloe Pickford between us, was already an IFBB pro – everyone else just had to catch up.

What I did with Chloe, and what you can do for yourself, is a slightly adjusted version of the idea of 'true self versus ideal self'.

This exercise involves imagining your ideal self in detail. Who is this person? What does this person do, where do they go, what have they achieved? What do they look like, what do they eat and drink, how do they sleep? Visualise that version of yourself and write it down. Now, identify where, who and what you are right now. Identify your current behaviours and attributes and write those down, right next to your ideal self. What you must now do is fill the gap between the two.

Say, for one extreme example, you want to be the chief executive officer (CEO) of the company you work for. What does your CEO wear, what do they eat, how do they carry themselves? What have they accomplished? How do they communicate? Take that information and *become* that yourself. Identify yourself as a CEO and use that language when speaking to yourself.

This is neurolinguistic programming (NLP), the theory that our language dictates our behaviour. NLP's foundation is that if a person speaks to themselves in a negative way then their behaviour is likely to be a reflection of that, and as a result they will struggle, be depressed and not achieve what they want to in their personal lives. Conversely, if a person speaks to themselves in an encouraging and positive way, they are far more likely to succeed. Remember the example of 'trying to quit' versus 'teetotal'? That's this process in action.

I'm not saying that you will become the CEO of your company just based on an identity shift – some goals take a lot of work of course. But how you perceive yourself also reflects to a degree how others see you. And if you carry yourself with the confidence of a CEO, if you embody that attitude, others will notice it. The confidence boost this gives you will improve your performance, the new habits you're forming around your work will become second nature and you are more likely to be perceived as someone who is ready for that next step in their career.

Our goals and resilience

Let's examine the idea that having a goal will enhance your resilience more closely. I've had a significant number of clients suffering from frustration and anxiety, not knowing why, but feeling very angry, nervous, sad and extremely wound up. The truth is that a lot of them feel this way because, ultimately, they have simply sat still for far too long.

We have to remember exactly what it is that we have evolved from. Cave people were designed to travel on foot for an average of 20 km a day. This was to benefit the tribe: to find food and hunt and fight for collective benefit and safety. We did this for thousands of years, the Paleolithic period was 2.5 million years ago, until 10,000 years BC. Later on, as civilisation developed, we pursued things to great and noble ends. We idolised the great men and women who shaped our very world – people like Boudica and Alexander the Great, Odysseus and Achilles – great powerhouses of people, heralded for their ingenuity, emotional fortitude and brilliance. We sang songs and read about their adventures and achievements, and we pushed and we continued to grow. We built great temples and infrastructures, we fought for our beliefs and against tyranny. In essence, we worshipped the idea of being overwhelmed and being successful in the face of it. As Thomas Babington Macaulay wrote, 'How can man die better, than facing fearful odds, for the ashes of his fathers, and the temples of his Gods?'[5]

This is perhaps a bit of a segue, but I have always found that *Love Island* really does epitomise the difference in how we are designed to live versus how we choose to live now. Bear with me because I will explain what I mean. *Love Island*, or other similar TV shows, is a great example of how Western society encourages individualisation over collectivism. The basis of the show appears to be picking a partner, but the actual purpose is to partner up with someone to win a prize – a big cash sum split between the winners. The partnership therefore becomes strategic and infused with an individualistic goal rather than a genuine connection, and easily dissolved if one of the partners becomes a weaker bet (although perhaps maybe some of them do fall in love, who knows!). This is really the opposite of how we're designed to live and nurture our relationships. Ideally, we live in closely bonded family units that support and care for each other so we can thrive in difficult conditions and build together.

Love Island is entertainment of course, and should not reflect real life, so it becomes a problem when young and impressionable people take it as an example of how they should behave towards a potential love interest.

This is in stark contrast to the collective support for the heroes of our history, like Odysseus and Achilles, Boudica and Alexander. The people, real or mythical, who have shaped humanity through seemingly impossible shows of endurance, brilliance and resilience. Paragons who have endured great responsibility and remained incorruptible, who were so unwavering in their beliefs to be held accountable to them. Great minds who have invented, built and devised ideas that lasted the test of time, by having a purpose and making their identity fit that purpose. Or at least, so the tales about their victories go. Historians and storytellers really weren't in the habit of highlighting failures as much back then. But the stories we tell matter. They show us what we take as examples.

Overwhelming comfort is a big issue. Everything can be made infinitely easier, so why struggle for anything? As human beings in the Western world we simply couldn't imagine walking 20 km a day or sacrificing our well-being for the benefit of the tribe. Most of us wouldn't even consider shooting our own dinner and dragging it back to our house. We don't carve our own spoons or make our own bowls, we don't make fires in our backyards to roast our kill and we don't fight wolves to stop them from eating our young. And why would you choose that life anyway? Why would any of us? Netflix keeps us entertained, Deliveroo keeps us fed, Amazon delivers anything to our door that we might need within a day. Life really is easy compared to thousands of years ago. But intrinsically, as humans, it can be awful for us.

This perpetual comfort works for a very limited time before we start becoming disgruntled, and we start wanting to forego these instant releases of dopamine and instead try to achieve something more. This is why I argue that, contrary to what many people might think, younger generations are not lazier than older ones, but rather we are advancing at such a rate that simply what we ask them to achieve now is very different from what was expected a few generations ago. So how do you become 'great' when there are now so many definitions, different iterations and manifestations of that word? How do you challenge yourself when there are a hundred different ways to do so?

In the end, it comes down to stepping out of your comfort zone. If you're lucky enough to have grown up with comfort and privilege, there won't be much that forces you to do so. Consider the conscripts who stormed the beaches at D-Day – they really didn't have a choice. It was war, national defence was critical for survival, it *had* to be done. Consider the suffragettes, abolitionists, civil rights leaders. Oppression, abuse and tyranny are not acceptable in any civilised society, so the fight against the power structures that oppressed these people *had* to be fought and continues to be fought to this day – a prime example of mental resilience if there ever was one. All of these are examples of how goals that are fuelled by a 'why', by a sense of purpose and a strong identity, lead to mental resilience and fulfilment.

Failing to succeed

A large part of having goals is failing to achieve them. And there is a lot to be learned from failure.

Failure is a complicated process. As humans, we often attach status and identity to the victories we have planned for ourselves or the expectations of success placed on us by high-achieving family members or peer groups. This relentless striving for excellence can lead to great feelings of inadequacy if expectations are not immediately met.

Our desire to succeed is a good thing because it furthers the survival of the tribe. In our modern society, humans that strived for greatness are the reason why we have advanced at such a rate: curing diseases, building sky scrapers, devising theories of relativity, sculpting great works of art, and millions more examples of human brilliance. It is easy to look at these successes and the people who made them happen and believe ourselves to be inadequate and inferior to them. We don't tend to consider that they themselves have failed on their way to success.

There are, of course, lots of famous examples of this. Colonel Saunders (yes, the KFC guy) was famously rejected by 1009 restaurants for his fried chicken franchise idea before he found a backer. Dr Seuss was rejected by 27 different publishing houses before he was eventually successful. Famously Albert Einstein was expelled from school and refused entry to the Zurich Polytechnic School and is now renowned as being one of the greatest minds to have ever lived. He even once said 'Success is failure in progress.'

The point here is that all these people consistently continued to strive to achieve their goals. So then, if consistency is a key to success, perhaps it is time to do away entirely with the word 'failure', as from every single pursuit there are only three outcomes:

*

Outcome 1: We are successful. The qualification is achieved, the exam passed, the promotion earned, the house bought, the trophy lifted, whatever the context, you have won. Hurray!

Outcome 2: Not yet. You're not ready. You have to go away and practise more, rework, relearn, grow, be bigger, stronger, and gain more knowledge to come back with more skills and more practice. Whatever it is, you need to retreat and work. Being able to see what needs improvement is key to becoming better, and being able to separate your ego from your performance is key to this. Not seeing criticism as a personal attack is a difficult skill to master, especially if you're personally passionate about what you do. But understand that your response to criticism is a reflection of yourself and that your ability to learn from it is a fantastic skill to have and is an almost guaranteed road to success. Understand what you need to improve and improve it.

Outcome 3: This is not where you need to be. Hear me out. I am not a believer in fate, I believe I make my own, so I am not suggesting that there is a higher power trying to guide you to something else. What I am trying to say is that if you pour all your passion, effort and time into a thing, over and over again, and that thing continuously doesn't work out with no measurable improvement, then you might not be doing the right thing for you. If it were the right thing, then all your time, effort and talent would eventually lead you to success. Forcing yourself to be something that you are not won't bring you success, it will bring you misery and failure. Assessing this takes complete honesty with yourself, and it is very hard to learn. You need to be able to critically assess whether what you're doing, if you keep doing it, will lead to a different outcome. You need to ask yourself, 'Will achieving this bring me true fulfilment?' and be honest with your answer. You need to learn where the point to stop is, when enough is enough. I almost died trying to pass SAS selection, and pushing my body to that point and then not passing made me realise it wasn't for me. Leaving it behind led me to explore new avenues, new ideas, new passions, and I find myself where I am now: writing a book, helping people with their mental health, being a dad, studying at university and running a business. Not everything you attempt to do is meant for you, and that's okay. Learning where your real talents lie through trial and error will help you find what brings you intrinsic fulfilment.

If you can fully embrace this concept – that you are learning by failing, that the neural patterns in your head form around the arrival of new information, that they correct themselves and change and strengthen in this process – then you will understand that failure is an opportunity to learn and grow, and in turn become resilient.

How to achieve your goals using MIND

I've already covered a few methods to make it easier to achieve your goals. Now, here is how you can use the MIND method to fortify that pillar.

Measured success

We tend to look forward only and focus on the next goal, the next certificate, qualification or success. We plan for it and look at it and once there, often move past it with little to no recognition for ourselves for what we have achieved and done. Ask yourself, how often do you take a moment to sit and enjoy the wonderful things that you are capable of? How often do you make time to celebrate the things you have achieved and worked so hard to bring to fruition? How often have you said, 'I am proud of me and what I have done?' I would suggest, the answer is rarely. We often struggle to acknowledge our own triumphs, worrying instead that we are ourselves showboats or arrogant for even mentioning it. We become dismissive of ourselves, and we even go so far as to undermine our own achievements. You have to stop that right now. See your success and that who and what you are is a culmination of brilliance and opportunity. The sooner you can identify the successes that you have created in your life, the sooner you can see and measure that success.

Intrinsic motivation

Identity is the most powerful tool to creating behavioural change that I know. If you can change your identity to fit your purpose, then your reliance on motivation disappears entirely. I go to the gym every day, even on a rest day I go to do some 'active recovery' (very light cardio and stretching). I've repeated this action so much that not doing it creates emotional distress to me. I *have* to go, I *have* to train, I *have* to do it because it is a massive part of my identity. I have performed this positive behaviour so much that it requires zero motivation. This is why a body-builder making motivational videos makes no sense to me. Isn't it already who they are? They love it and get great reward from it, it's not someone doing something that they hate because they know they have to do it. This is why I have far greater feelings of affection and admiration for people who are just at the start of this journey of redefining themselves, especially if they face serious health struggles or other challenges which make shifting their identity that much more complicated. But this remains true: the key is identity. Make it who you are, and you need no motivation.

Now, in the present

Who you are now is a brilliant person with everything at your disposal to become any great thing that you want. There is nothing inherently 'wrong' with you. We are all flawed humans, and we all want to achieve great things. It's possible to have great belief in what you will become and also appreciate the work and effort required to achieve it without reflecting this back onto yourself in a negative way. Enjoying doing this work now and watching yourself grow is actually an essential part of building towards success. Humans have an incredible neurological response when attempting to achieve a task, which can be observed, and has been by the brilliant Robert Sapolsky in his book *Behave*.[6] We get huge spikes of dopamine in anticipation of reward, rather than in receipt of it. So, humans have evolved to enjoy work, to a certain degree at least. Of course, the allure of the sofa, snacks and streaming services creates desire to abandon our dreams and retreat to safety and comfort. Instead of giving in to this, hold on to the idea that there is enjoyment from working hard and consistently, even if in the moment it doesn't feel like it. As a result, you'll find yourself achieving more than ever before. It is as simple as this: a person who enjoys running will run for far longer than the individual simply running for a certain distance.

Dream big

'Realistic' goal setting frustrates me. Individuals with a negative self-belief will often find themselves setting goals that are so incredibly belittling to them. They undercut themselves because what they believe themselves to be capable of is so short of what they can actually do. Your success rests entirely on what you believe you can do. So, dream big, and then dream a little bigger. Our brains learn by a process called neuroplasticity. We rewire and reprogramme neurons to make new thought patterns, including memory, functional cognitive skills and emotions. So far, the limit to the brain's ability to do this is not understood. Essentially, we are all the same genetic blobs of potential, and if you consider yourself incapable of learning then that will be reflected in your behaviour. If you understand that your brain grows in the same way as everyone else's then its potential becomes limitless. So again, dream big, and dream authentically. What appeals to you? What will bring you fulfilment? Go do that thing. Your dreams exist for you, so why make them small?

Exercises

Exercise 1: The Wall of Self

This is a great exercise for pushing you further and reinforcing your identity. I call it the 'Wall of Self'.

When we were kids, our achievements and moments of growth were generally far more visibly celebrated. And if you have kids now, this exercise will likely also be familiar to you. Remember when your parents would hang up a picture that you'd done, perhaps made of macaroni or nondescript splashes of paint? Or if you won a prize, whether that was a medal or a trophy or a ribbon, and they'd find a place to proudly display it? Karate certificates, great report cards and swimming badges were lovingly stuck to the fridge or on a corkboard, inventions, creations and achievements, all moments of growth that were clearly lovingly celebrated.

As adults, we stopped doing this. This is really, really sad. As we get older, we lose that childlike wonder of the world and this sense of pride. We stop celebrating ourselves and our achievements.

So how do you stop becoming a downtrodden version of yourself? I have the remedy. Recreate that wall of achievements for yourself as an adult. Dig out your old academic degree and apprenticeship diplomas, your professional certificates, your artwork, sports trophies, photographs of great moments in your life, anything that you can be proud of, and stick them on your wall.

These memories of achievement will serve as a reminder of who you are and what you are capable of. They will reaffirm that identity you want to adopt as someone who has the ability to achieve their goals. And when you're having a wobble, this will help you stay on your path because you know you can push through – after all, you've done it before. I looked at my wall recently when I was exhausted from work and still had another essay to write for my degree. I've used it when I've felt myself come up with excuses for not going to the gym, or when I have a pile of emails to respond to and paperwork to fill in. My Wall of Self reminds me who I am, the steps that I'm taking to achieve a goal, what that goal is and why I'm trying to achieve it.

It's so important that this wall is personal to you. This is not about creating a (painfully) generic motivational message, like posters that say 'keep going' or 'hang in there'. This is about reminding you of your achievements and what you, as you are, are capable of. And if you do get that voice in your head that says you can't do it, look at your wall again and respond, 'Says who?' and carry on.

Exercise 2: True self and ideal self

I have a great exercise to help you identify the actions that you need to take you to where you want to be. As discussed, the best way to achieve your goals is to embody them and shift your identity to fit that purpose. This exercise is not in any way a method to somehow make you feel bad about yourself now or to eradicate the person you are now. This is about positive action.

Draw a line down the centre of a blank sheet of paper. At the top of the left-hand column, write 'True self' and at the top of the right-hand column, write 'Ideal self'. Now think about what you want to achieve. For instance, let's say you're pursuing a promotion at work. Under 'Ideal self' write down the characteristics of the version of you that has got this promotion. What's their attitude like, what are their beliefs and what kind of behaviours do they display? What kind of skills does this person have, how do they look and speak? Now, under 'True self', for each of the things you've listed, write down where you are now in comparison to the idealised version of yourself.

There's one rule here: you have to be objective about your current situation. It's easy to write about yourself in a negative way here and make it look as if you're nowhere near the ideal version of yourself. But that's often not the case, and you owe it to yourself to make an accurate assessment of the current version of yourself.

The point of this exercise is to identify the gaps between the facets of yourself that you want to change to become this ideal self. Writing it out like this will help you formulate a plan which you can actively work on to bring yourself closer to your ideal self.

It will also shift your perspective and make this ideal version of yourself much more achievable. It will no longer seem like a distant, impossible goal – instead, because you've identified the steps you need to take, becoming this person will be that much easier.

This is ultimately what I think manifestation is. It's not a matter of envisioning a future and believing in it so much that it magically happens. It's not about creating a vision board with pictures representing all the things you want and shouting affirmations at yourself in the mirror. This is a version of manifestation where you come up with a game plan with concrete steps that you can take to get you closer to your goal. It's the opposite of fooling yourself into believing that just because you think you deserve something it will be given to you. Life is not that easy. If you want it, find out what the steps are to get it, believe in yourself and go and fight for it.

Summary

There is great power in forging a new identity. It's far more effective than traditional goal setting. Identifying who you want to become and challenging your sense of self to become that person makes you far more likely to succeed. You too can push your limits and work on becoming what you dream of being.

Achieving your goals is not about obsessing over the idea of being in that end state. Instead it is about embracing the work you need to do and loving the effort that it takes. It's about the ups and downs of life that hinder, shift, delay or block the achievement of our goals and not letting this destroy our mental resilience. If you adopt the identity of a person who has achieved their goal, you maintain that sense of resilience and motivation on the way to success. Be unshakeable in this belief in yourself, and maintain the belief that you are capable.

We learn our lessons in defeat. It is an opportunity to learn about ourselves, to grow and to ensure that we are on the right path. In that sense, there is no such thing as failure. You will always gain something from the times you're unsuccessful. Carry this as faith and apply it to your dreams. If you do this, I have no doubt that you will build your resilience with great success.

CHAPTER FIVE

Relationships

What you can expect to learn in this chapter:

- The importance of the people that surround you.
- The relationship with yourself.
- Boundaries and how to set them.
- The detrimental effect of toxic relationships.

I am heading to the top floor of a town house. I am 17 years old. My Metallica hoodie is ripped, with small burn holes from the weed I regularly smoke. My jeans are disgustingly filthy, as are my shoes. I am a few days into a bender, without cleaning my teeth, and my hair is a disgraceful mass of grease and VO5 wet-look gel.

I was escorted onto the premises by someone I would consider a friend, and occasionally, an employer. The friends I arrived with are waiting outside, bashfully, since I am the only one allowed in. The town house doesn't look too bad on the outside, but if you look closely you can see the reinforced windows, the coded doors to get in and out, the security cameras, and the distinct look of a halfway house. This halfway house is for the homeless, the prison leavers and other vulnerable members of society.

There is the unmistakable smell of burning plastic on my way up, which really hits the back of my throat. It's the smell of someone cooking heroin. I'm nearly at the top floor, where the smell is more pungent. I am the only one trusted to go into this drugs den. Because that's exactly what this is, and I am in here to score. I have enough money for some coke, and a couple of lads want pills too.

I'm holding my nerve as I walk into the top-floor bedroom. Caps cover grey faces, the movements of these men in there are slow but controlled. I'm suddenly very aware that I am very robbable, and there's very little I can do about it if it does happen. What would I explain to the police or ambulance service if I got hurt here? 'Yeah, mate, I wanted to get wrecked, and that happened, just not in the way that I'd hoped.' I can't do anything. There are four men here, and desperate people are dangerous people.

The room pauses, waiting for me to be introduced to them, and soon I hope, as they look keen to kick me out. The lad who took me in and up the stairs, says, 'Here, Jelly's safe.' The room relaxes slightly on hearing my school nickname, and the confirmation that I'm no threat.

One of the men, I reckon in his early twenties, is using a lighter to heat a spoon. I don't have the proper adjectives to describe what his face looks like – he is fucked. That's the only word for it. Grey skin pulled tight across bones, the exhaustion in his eyes suggesting he hasn't slept deeply in years, with a complexion implying he hasn't been fed properly in years either. His body language and movements suggest he doesn't feel safe or loved, and probably never has his entire life. I am both scared of him and deeply sympathetic toward him. I have no idea what has led him to this point, all I know is that heroin is serious, life-destroying shit.

The gear is handed over to me after I show my cash, and I exit the building, disappearing into the night with the people I arrived with. I call them 'friends' but that's steep. They were patiently waiting for me to get the drugs because I knew the guy who could get me in. He used to sell me weed. One time, another bloke I knew decided not to pay him for quite a lot of weed. I knew where the bloke lived, so the dealer and I went to his house, and the dealer pulled a gun on him. The guy paid him the money and the dealer gave me half. It turned out the gun was a replica, but Jesus did it look real and menacing. After that, I had a golden ticket to go where the really desperate members of our society would hide and to buy any drugs I wanted, as if this was some badge of honour.

I took so much ecstasy that night and did so much cocaine that I chewed the inside of my cheeks to rags and absolute bloody ruin. I had apparently tried to climb out of a window several times and had several huge chunks shaved out of the side of my hair.

I used to go wild with drugs and alcohol during that time of my life. I would really go out to damage myself. I would drink and smoke excessively to get away from who and what I was.

I was ashamed of my childhood. I was carrying this shame because my biological dad had gone to prison. This made me feel so overwhelmingly worthless. I had lost control, and I didn't care. It felt right. It was an escape. I didn't like, and certainly didn't love, any part of myself. And this was my first encounter with suicidal thoughts.

I was in a spiral. I had some good friends who would encourage me and believed that I could do better, but I also had 'friends' who would seriously encourage this incredibly dangerous behaviour.

More than once I had found myself sleeping rough. Not just curled up on a bench after one beer too many on a night out, but curled up on a bench with literally nowhere else to go. Things were so incredibly difficult at my mum's. The inevitable blowouts between me and my mum meant I wasn't always able to stay with her. I once even paid to sleep on a sofa at my old boss's really awful flat. I would get myself into such states, with nowhere to go, that sleeping on a bench, in a doorway or slumped up in a garden felt like the only choice.

I have been involved with some extremely desperate people, men so twisted by the hand they feel they were dealt in life that they would rob and hurt those around them. I very much associated with that. I thought I was a bad man at the time. I thought I was becoming a version of my biological father, an idea I hated and resented so much. I would feel a physical pain to think about him, like a twisting in my stomach. Yet here I was, being him. Violent, angry and hedonistic. The life I led was about getting drunk, the next hit of drugs, the next way to escape.

I was disappearing off grid from my good friends at the positive places in my life, like my local rugby club, to commit increasingly dangerous acts of what was effectively self-harm and abuse through self-destructive behaviour. I was so depressed, and I was filled with so much self-loathing, that I can't even quantify to myself now how terrible I felt.

Poor mental health takes so many shapes, feels like so many different emotions, causes so many complications. You don't know how to even begin to describe the pain, the confusion, the physiological response of perpetual anxiety. I literally lacked the language skills to accurately describe how I felt.

One day, I thought about that lad I saw taking heroin. I was staying on someone's sofa again because I had nowhere else to go. I had drunk a large bottle of vodka, wet myself and been sick. My host took my clothes off me and pulled me into bed naked because she wanted 'cuddles'. I was effectively paralytic. I had sick all down me. I couldn't manage to find or use the language to explain how uncomfortable her actions made me, nor did I have the capacity to defend myself against what was happening. I was a wreck and there was very little that I could do to stop it.

The next morning, I threw up after I'd smoked a roll up without a filter and thought, *I have got to get out of here*. I felt like that lad I'd seen – powerless to the destructive forces around me, hopeless and vulnerable. I had to make a change. Two days later, I walked into the Army recruitment office, and my entire life changed forever.

We need the right people around us

There is a huge amount of scientific research that asserts the fact that our relationships with other people have a tremendous effect on our mental resilience. Bad relationships specifically degrade our well-being. Our relationships are a crucial factor in the formation of our personality, especially in childhood when our brains are malleable. Freud was a pioneer in this area, and his papers on childhood development are now supported by neuroscientific research.[1]

There are also some brilliant studies that show how lack of relationships negatively affect our well-being. It's so interesting to see how we, as humans, crave a tribe, and when we're unsuccessful in finding one, we become lonely and quite possibly even ill. That's right, a 2015 study on loneliness by Julianne Holt-Lunstad and colleagues at Brigham Young University in Utah actually concluded that loneliness is a massive contributor to premature death.[2] This study of 3.4 million people showed that people who were living in social isolation have a 30 per cent chance of dying prematurely – similar to the rates for obesity and smoking. It is also worth noting here that in 2018, the UK Government instated a 'minister of loneliness' as part of a strategy to combat loneliness, especially in the elderly, carers and people who had lost loved ones.[3] This is important, because being lonely literally increases your chance of death.

We crave a tribe, we crave company, but it has to be the right company. Another study, conducted by Debra Umberson and Jennifer Karas Montez in 2010, revealed that people with unsatisfactory relationships are far more likely to suffer from chronic disease and poor health.[4] So, isolation and bad relationships both affect your health negatively.

The last few years we've seen the 'rise of the introvert', with more people identifying with this personality trait and books being published about the virtues of introversion. There is nothing inherently wrong with introversion, but don't confuse it with isolating yourself – they are two different things. Needing and taking time for yourself and being someone who prefers to think about things quietly on your own is fine, but never seeing or speaking to another soul is not. If you've been burned by bad relationships in the past, whether friendships, romantic or even your own family, retreating into solitude might feel like a safe option, but research shows it really isn't. Instead, you need to look for the people who are right for you.

This leads me very nicely into the adage 'your vibe attracts your tribe'. It sounds cheesy, but there is an actual neurobiological process for this. Let's look this more closely.

Your 'vibe' is built through your behaviours, meaning what people observe you say and do, how you carry yourself and how you communicate and behave in your environment. From your pursuit of education, your hobbies, the sports you play, how you approach your health, work and so on, people can see what your values are and how you behave in these environments. Earlier in the book we explored how we recognise behaviours of others and the subconscious responses that this generates. How a person carries themselves (which, to get back to an earlier point, is also informed by our caregivers) will be recognised by others who carry themselves in a similar way. Recognising this behaviour makes us feel safe, and we're more likely to communicate with people who we perceive to be similar to us. That connection to another person is encouraged and maintained with a powerful combination of serotonin – your mood-regulating hormone, dopamine – your reward hormone, and oxytocin –, the 'love' hormone we produce in order to bond with others.

There are many examples of people just picking up on their 'tribe'. Ex-military people always somehow manage to find each other because the way that they carry themselves reminds them of something familiar and warm. People who come from the same towns with similar accents and who use the same turns of phrase somehow find themselves sitting next to each other and conversing. This is easily mistaken as an external power guiding you – 'it's fate we should meet!' But it is not fate. It's your subconscious looking for what is safe and what it recognises. A lot of studies confirm this neurological process.[5]

This is something that you can absolutely use to your advantage, and it's one of the reasons it's so important that you are brave and choose to be true to yourself and live authentically. If you pretend to be someone you're not, you won't attract the people who will actually be good for you. I suggest that you go and 'vibe' in an environment that you're comfortable with. Be you, be brilliant, and others who recognise this will be drawn to you.

Behaviour modelling

As we've learned, the hippocampus, our emotional memory bank, is shaped by our childhood. We learn from the experiences we have and events we witness as a child. But what happens if those are negative experiences generated by terrible people? What if the relationships you experience as a child are violent, invalidating and abusive? Then that will be a cause of huge detriment to your mental resilience.

The information that you are given from your caregivers is often what you believe to be true. If you never experienced the much-needed nurturing and soothing from your caregivers then, understandably, you will become overwhelmed by adversity because you haven't learned how to nurture and soothe yourself. We can see that neural patterns are negatively affected by exposure to abuse. Emotional regulation and cognitive function are disrupted by early traumatic childhood experiences.

Moreover, our childhood relationships tend to define the proverbial yardstick by which we measure all our adult relationships. How our mothers treat us is how we expect other women we become intimate with to treat us. How our fathers treat us is how we learn to expect other men that we become intimate with to treat us. Friendships that our parents have are an example to us of how to behave towards our friends.

This of course leads to an inherent problem, what if they were all terrible people? What if they were twats to each other? What if they were twats to us? What if they were insecure idiots who at every opportunity undermined and belittled us, because the prospect of our success is like looking into a mirror of their own inadequacy and their own perceptions of failure? What if they never learned compassion? What if they had zero emotional intelligence? What if they had no life experience or wealth of worldly knowledge and education to draw on to help support and guide us?

Imagine what that does to the foundations of your mental resilience. Imagine how much that can turn you against yourself. Now you can see how negative early relationships will have a terrible effect on your mental resilience. If you are told and shown that you are incapable, you will believe that you are incapable of even the simplest of tasks, let alone big ones. If you believe that your mother doesn't love you as a child, you will grow up believing you are not worthy of love. What your caregivers tell you, how they communicate with you, is how you'll communicate with yourself. So how are you supposed to live up to what you could be if you've inherited these beliefs about yourself? How you express love comes from childhood, your internal dialogue comes from childhood, and your expectations from friends, lovers and siblings come from childhood.

My experiences as a child serve as an example that we can break the cycle of negative behaviour modelled to us by caregivers. I saw so much violence and anger in my childhood that it affected my self-esteem, identity and belief in myself. However, I've chosen to never let my daughter get infected with this negativity, and instead set a positive example for her. Instead of the rage and explosions of anger I was shown, I show her kindness, consideration and humour, and this is the behaviour she copies. Modelling positive behaviours like this when you come from a place that has emotionally crippled your development isn't easy, but this is how trauma cycles are broken – by recognising negative patterns you've inherited and consciously changing them. This way I can ensure that she doesn't learn the same things I was taught.

I've written a lot now about abusive relationships, but of course not all negative relationships are abusive. A lot of people around us simply lack emotional intelligence. Everyone has their own fears, trials and terrible examples of caregivers. Everyone, to a certain degree, is broken and confused, lost and angry, and projecting that onto others. Projection occurs when a person takes an internal belief and applies it to themselves without questioning its truth. Often, people project with little or no thought of the consequences of how their actions and statements appear, sound or look.

A pretty innocuous example of projection is when a caregiver shouts 'Be careful!' to a child as they run off to play in a park with their friends. This seems like a perfectly parental thing to tell a child, but what you're actually doing is projecting. You're communicating to them the fears you have about the world, based on the information you have gained and the experiences that you've had. The child, very likely, does not have these fears yet, but in that moment you are telling them that the world is a scary place, that there are things to be feared, that people can be dangerous, that they might hurt themselves. Of course, this is kind of valid – children are naive and should to a degree be made aware of the dangers of the world. But they lack context, and overwhelming children with fear of all the scary things out there, which you as an adult can compartmentalise, will only lead to them becoming fearful.

Another emotionally unintelligent thing people do is invalidating others. This, again, can be especially noticeable in parental relationships with children. Some parents do not involve their children in important life decisions, such as moving house to a different location, which means the child has to leave behind their social life and the places they're comfortable in. This may communicate to the child that what they feel about the situation isn't important or valid.

Another way of emotionally invalidating others is by not respecting their emotional responses. In a carer/child relationship, this might manifest itself in such exclamations as 'Stop crying, or I'll give you something to cry about!' 'You're overreacting, you're making a mountain out of a molehill.' Again, the child learns from this that their responses aren't valid, that their emotions are worthless, as if the pain that they're feeling is irrelevant, incorrect or an overreaction. This bleeds into adult relationships, where some people struggle to express to others how they feel and then invalidate themselves internally and disregard their feelings for someone else's priorities. The taught behaviours and experiences we've had growing up are the very foundations of a resilient mindset, on which our Relationships pillar is based. The path to developing this pillar and our mental resilience involves an honest assessment of our current relationships as adults.

Toxic relationships versus healthy relationships

The term 'toxic relationship' is thrown around a lot nowadays, but what does this actually mean? I often see it used by people to refer to relationships that no longer suit them or their demands, or that they are simply having a hiccup with. Or, I see people using 'toxic' in reference to other people as a way to deflect from the fact that they should actually be looking inward and taking ownership of their own behaviour. So, let's define what toxic and healthy relationships really look like. These six signs are applicable to all relationships, whether familial, friendly, professional or romantic. Let's start with the traits of a toxic relationship.

1. **You no longer feel (or have never felt) respected.** This indicates that this person does not respect your boundaries, even when you have set them very clearly (more on that at the end of this chapter). You have told them clearly what you need from them, and they are not meeting that. They have little to no regard for how something they do or say will make you feel and take no accountability for the effect on you. We have covered what emotional intelligence means, and we know that a facet of emotional intelligence is understanding how your behaviour makes others feel. If a person understands that their behaviour makes you feel incredibly uncomfortable and they continue to do it anyway, they are choosing to do so.

2. **You feel on edge around them.** Your nervous system will tell you when it's picking up on something worrying or sensing danger. When a person's attitude, behaviours or beliefs are challenging your sense of safety (and that includes emotional safety), your subconscious will let you know. Your hippocampus will recognise their behaviours as dangerous, and you will feel tense and uncomfortable around them. This is your intuition, and you should *listen to it*. Every time I've ignored my intuition, the outcome has been terrible. Always ask yourself what your body is trying to tell you and why it is trying to tell you it. Be aware, of course, of hypervigilance based on trauma, but once that's assessed try to understand the source of your physiological reaction to this stimulus. If it's still there, and a person makes you feel on edge by being around them, then deny them your presence.

3. **You bring out the worst in each other.** Being around this person is bringing out a side to you that you do not like. This is not an opportunity to attribute your behaviours to someone else, though, and tell yourself it's not your fault or that you're not somehow responsible for how you act. Rather, this is an opportunity to tell yourself firmly, 'I do not like who I am when I am around this person, it's time to leave.' I see lots of couples being overly competitive and derogatory to each other. If you are not supporting and bringing out the best in the other person then this is a very concerning sign.

4. **Your self-esteem takes the brunt of it.** Over time, you start to think less of yourself and think more self-deprecating thoughts. Perhaps through derogatory comments, sneaky remarks or actions of disrespect, this person has started to trample you down, and it starts to erode your self-esteem. You somehow feel worth less than before you knew them, simply by being around this person. They make you feel terrible about yourself, you start blaming yourself more and become more submissive.

5. **You are giving more than you are getting back.** You feel as if you're shouldering an unfair amount of the work it requires to maintain the relationship. This has to be a recurring pattern, as relationships do ebb and flow, we get busy, our friends, family or partners get busy, and we don't always have the same amount of time and energy to put into them. But if you feel that you're consistently putting in more effort than the other person, that you're the one who always has to text, organise, show up, give emotional support and deal with their problems and you're not getting this in return, you are more committed to the relationship than they are. This can produce feelings of rejection and of being unwanted. This may inspire you to

set new boundaries and establish exactly what is required of both of you through clear communication, or it might cause you to work even harder, to the point of exhibiting increasingly desperate and demeaning behaviours to try to suit the other person's demands and get their validation, while sidelining your own needs.

6. **Physical, emotional or sexual abuse.** This is the big one, and you should pay very close attention to the warning signs of abuse. There is so much to say about this topic and I'm aware a bullet point does not suffice to cover it. Physical assault is never okay. Emotional manipulation, degrading behaviour, gaslighting, abusive name-calling and anything else that falls under emotional abuse is never okay. Any form of sexual contact without your consent is never okay. Abuse can also be more subtle and manifest over longer periods when a person has started to wear you down and affected your self-esteem and self-worth. Trust your intuition here. People who treat you like this belong in a toilet, and you belong somewhere safe. Leave. Now.

Now, these are the six markers of a healthy relationship:

1. **You feel respected.** The people around you know what your boundaries are, they know what you need and they are willing to compromise their behaviour to meet them.
2. **You feel comfortable around them.** You can be authentic, vulnerable, open and yourself around them. You can belly laugh, cry, share and grow without fear of judgement, and within their company you find great courage.
3. **You bring out the best in each other.** They make you feel supported, and you achieve more by having that person in your corner. When you're at your lowest, that's who you can call.

4. They have a positive influence on your self-esteem. They believe in you, and you see that clearly, which in turn builds your self-esteem. You are more confident when you're with them.

5. You give equally. You both put consistent effort into the relationship and contribute equally to its maintenance, its growth and fixing any issues.

6. The love is unconditional. This doesn't mean that you love each other despite abuse, it means that you know that you can set a boundary, express your needs, that you can have a disagreement or even an argument, and you know they still love you. Being clear about your boundaries does not make you feel frozen out or as if you're at risk of losing the relationship. They understand who you are, and they love you all the more for your honesty. Even if you go through a difficult time, you know that they still love you.

It is well worth watering the flowers of a good relationship to make it bloom, rather than focusing all your attention on the ones that are wilting. Healthy relationships impact our mental resilience positively, and toxic relationships will erode it. That being said, the most important relationship that you should be assessing this way is the one you have with yourself.

When assessing the relationships in your life, do keep in mind that everyone has the capability to grow. How you are now is not how you will always be, and you can choose better. The people around you can do the same, but this has to be a choice on their part too.

Weeding out toxic relationships becomes especially challenging when it comes to family.

I can hear all overbearing and manipulative parents cry 'blood is thicker than water!' Well, some people claim that the full quote is actually 'the blood of the covenant is thicker than the water of the womb', and I like this interpretation much better. The people you choose to be in your life are arguably more important than the family you're born into.

This is especially true for those of us who come from toxic family backgrounds. There's a term I like, 'family of choice', which is the counterpart to 'family of origin'. It's a term used especially in the LGBTQA+ community, whose members often face rejection and ostracism from their birth families. In that community, they find the people who embrace them for who they are, who become their 'family of choice'. It's sad and unjust that this has to happen at all, but being able to pick your own family is a beautiful thing.

The idea that you choose who to be in your life over the people you happen to be related to is an uncomfortable truth for families that enable each other's terrible behaviours and attitudes. I have seen this multiple times, from a variety of perspectives: grandparents projecting the terrible childhood they endured onto their children, who as parents then project onto you, and you in turn may project onto your own children.

It's not just families though; toxic friendships and romantic engagements feed your own negative internal dialogue and are absolutely destructive to your emotional resilience. How can you ever push through adversity and learn the necessary lessons required of you to succeed and grow if you are made to feel unworthy and useless by the very people appointed to support and encourage you?

Here's one important thing to remember: you don't actually owe anyone a relationship. You don't owe them your time, or your emotional energy. The only person you owe anything to is yourself. If people mistreat or even abuse you, deny them access to the most expensive commodity that you have: your time. Remember, if something costs you your peace, it has become too expensive.

Keep in mind, however, that this is a two-way street, and nobody owes you a relationship either. If you are unable to put your pride to one side and accept that your behaviour has made someone feel a certain way, this is the exact same emotional response you would be offended by, and you shouldn't be surprised if you're cut out for behaviours that you would cut others out for too.

I really dislike it when people are hurtful to others and hide behind the cliché 'I'm just being honest'. You're not being honest, you're being cruel. Clear feedback is kind, but cruel feedback is not. There are different ways to word difficult things to the people you care about, and choosing the easy way and cutting someone down shows your lack of emotional maturity. You can be candid and upfront about how something makes you feel without being a dick about it, and how you choose to word something is still always a reflection of you. You don't 'say things as they are' you actually 'say things as *you* are'. Your words and reactions to the world around you are how you broadcast who you are: your personality, experiences, insecurities and perceptions of your own inadequacy that are all on display. Be very wary of how you choose to criticise people. Make sure that you are not projecting your own mistreatment from childhood onto your relationships. If you struggle with this, try to be more aware of your emotional responses to stimuli and remember you can always rely on the FOCUS method from the Emotional Intelligence chapter to help you manage those responses.

Building your Relationships pillar is a two-way street. You have to be able to rely on others to build this pillar, and equally, they have to rely on you to build theirs. Positive, healthy relationships involve effort from more than the one person. If you are not being supportive and empathetic to others, then in turn your Relationships pillar will suffer too.

How to nurture your relationships using MIND

Luckily, because of neuroplasticity, most counterproductive things we've learned about how we interact with others can be unlearned. Having a healthy, steady Relationships pillar is incredibly important to mental resilience, and nurturing your relationships is a huge part of maintaining this pillar. This is how the MIND method can help you with this.

Measured success

This is a tricky one – how do we actually measure a fulfilling relationship? Is it a relationship that allows you to be authentic, that allows you to speak openly without fear of retaliation, that allows for criticism and growth and compromise? The answer to this is something that only you can ever possibly know. I would suggest that here you check in with how you feel. We often feel differently around people who are healthy and supportive than we do around people who are toxic to us. We feel energised and excited to see them and look forward to being around them. This is a feeling that you should be actively looking for in your relationships, rather than dreading to see them and feeling drained afterwards.

In terms of measuring the success of your relationships, you must consider the feelings you have around the people in your life and observe where you are now compared to where you were before. Check in regularly, perhaps every six months, and ask yourself: 'How do I feel around these people?' Can you see a change in your relationships? That hanging out with the 'wrong crowd' cliché of adolescence – does that still apply, or have you now, as an adult, surrounded yourself with people who want the best for you? What does your friendship group feel like now? Can you be yourself without dimming the parts of your personality that risk highlighting the inadequacy of others? Have you been able to set boundaries with people, and are they respected? As children, we often find ourselves wanting to fit in, willing to be someone that we are not to secure a place in a group; is this something that you are continuing now? Look to your relationships, who are you when you are with these people? If you're happy with your answer, you're on the right path.

Intrinsic motivation

Most people do have an intrinsic and deep-set desire to meet people who will elevate and educate them. Being motivated to have positive relationships in our life is an essential part of the human experience. Who we are and what we subjectively want to achieve is often built around the friendships that we make. This is one of the reasons I reject the concept of the 'self-made' millionaire, as this completely discards the relationships and friendships that have helped and encouraged that person along the way, not to mention their (possibly exasperated) partners who went out of their way to help them. We inevitably want to elevate our experiences and friends, which is why it's so important to have them around.

I know that the man I am is the product of the people I choose to be around. A great example of this is my friend Lee Soper, who so ferociously encouraged me to join Colchester Rugby Team and coach there (he actually got me the job). Throughout my life, he's lent me an ear and given solid advice about my career, my personal life and the mistakes I've made. Even as civilians, him with an enormous Gandalf style beard and towering 3 feet above everyone, he still supports and encourages me. I messaged him recently, after he insisted that I take a break from work and come see him for the gun salute to the Queen, saying, 'Thank you for all you do for me, I'd be lost without you, mate', to which he replied, 'That's what family is for.' There is great strength in that support, from people of the same mindset, travelling to a similar destination or just being in your corner. It makes you want to work so much harder towards your goals. Your people will motivate you and will help you achieve great things.

Now, in the present

In the process of interacting with people, it's hard to not be derailed by our own traumas and the subsequent expectations of others. I have personally been frustrated many times explaining to a potential partner that it is unfair of them to expect me to fix what another person has broken, that they must fix themselves and not project their pain from an old wound onto me. And as is natural with all humans, I've been guilty of this myself – angry at how an old relationship has broken down, I have projected my insecurity of this relationship onto the new person. This is something we must all work on. There is an element of learned behaviour here – our subconscious has absorbed our previous experiences and is making sure that we do not get hurt again, so we have a subconscious response to a behaviour that reminds us of a previous negative experience with another person. But you must remain present in your relationships. Remember who you're interacting with, right now – they're not the person who hurt you before, they are an entirely different human. It's fine to have these feelings, but you must take responsibility for how you choose to respond. Stay present when interacting with your people, do not be drawn into negative patterns that are so easy to repeat, simply because that's what you've always done. Instead, see every new relationship as a way to grow and move forward and break away from old patterns.

Dream big

Do this for you and for them. That's right – elevate your friends, your family, your co-workers, your teammates. Help them find the fulfilment that they deserve. If you find yourself in a position of power, pull them up with you where you can. Show them the love that they deserve. We are all ultimately in this game for the same thing: fulfilment. If you can dream big for yourself, you can dream big for others too. A large part of this work is actively forming useful connections: work on projects together, form plans together, talk to and support each other, pump each other up, collectively dream and plan. The key here is to figure out how you can help each other in a real way.

I did an experiment once with a group of ten service leavers who were on their way out of the Army. This involved each person stating where they were going to live, what their desired trade or employment was and what, if anything, they were worried about struggling to achieve. The results were fascinating – as each person expressed their concerns, there was somehow always someone in the group who knew of a way to help. The lad who mentioned he wanted to be a carpenter but worried about his lack of experience was matched with someone whose uncle worked in a large building firm, and so he set him up with contact details. Some people couldn't figure out how to fill out their veteran's railcard, and they immediately got help with this. People who were struggling to find a place to live were matched up with people who knew of a vacancy.

There is more available to you than you think – you simply need to ask. This is how clubs are formed, jobs are found, connections are made, opportunities are created, all without spending a single penny. It's just a genuine discussion about what your dreams are, and people wanting to help each other out. Whatever your dreams are, share them with your circle, and encourage them to do the same with you. There is very little that we can't achieve when acting collectively to support and grow with each other.

Exercises

Exercise 1: Assessing your circle and setting boundaries

The first thing you must learn to do is to assess how good for you the people in your immediate circle are. Thankfully, I have a three-step process to identify if the people in your circle are as supportive and invested in you as you are in them.

Step 1: How do you feel around them?

We have all grown up with completely different perspectives and biases of the world, therefore what we need to find fulfilment and enjoyment can be completely different. Establishing whether a relationship is meaningful and fulfilling isn't about identifying people who don't agree with you and banishing them to the shadow realm. Great minds don't think alike: great minds challenge and question each other. There is nothing worse than surrounding yourself with 'yes' men, and, equally, it's terrible to be surrounded by people who undercut you at every opportunity. Relationships begin and end with the connection that you have with the other person, so ask yourself this simple question: 'When I am around this person, how do I *feel?*'

Remember the messages that your body is sending you, your intuition? Follow this. Is it a good feeling? Does it feel easy, stress free and relaxing? Or does this person set your teeth on edge, do they make you nervous, as if you can't be yourself around them? If the feeling is negative, ask yourself why. Are you drawn to them because they are as potentially toxic and awful as someone from your childhood, and are you somehow trying to relive and 'fix' this relationship? Do you feel as if you somehow need validation from them because they make you feel bad about yourself? Are you worried they might deprive you of their friendship if you lay down boundaries, and does this stop you from being honest with them? If questions like these come up, it's time to start reconsidering this relationship.

Step 2: Do they give back?

This is such a common thing. We often find ourselves in relationships where we give far more than we get in return. This is not to be confused with people who rely on us for care and struggle to give back, whether temporarily (like a friend going through a rough patch of mental health) or permanently if you're a carer. Of course, you can't say, 'Sorry, Nan, but when was the last time that you bathed me?' and ditch her – that's not what this means. This is about understanding that there are people in the world more than happy to take from you because it is on constant offer. They expect your support and help and praise and to be at their every beck and call and yet do not ever give back. I am sure that you have personal experience of this, you have been around people who are inherently selfish or self-centred, and where you find yourself constantly reaching out and making sacrifices for the relationship, while they do not. It can be hard to let go of these people, as any relationship falling apart can feel like rejection, even if it's a natural thing as your perspectives on the world and what a friendship should look like have grown apart. But it's important, because you can't keep looking after people who don't look after you. Your resilience will fall apart if you feed everyone else from your plate and leave nothing for yourself.

Step 3: Set boundaries

The single biggest provider of peace in your life is teaching everybody in it how to treat you. You have every right to stand up for yourself if you feel someone has behaved in a way that makes you uncomfortable. That's right, even if you were brutally and continually invalidated as a child and struggle to speak up, you too have every right to defend the boundaries of what you do and do not find acceptable behaviour. I can feel some of you tremble as you read this, but it is true. In fact, boundaries aren't just helpful to a relationship, they are *essential* to it. You must absolutely set boundaries with people, because if you don't, it becomes difficult to be upset with people for not respecting them, as they simply don't know what they are.

Setting boundaries is a complicated process and one that's difficult to master if you've never been taught. Say someone speaks to you in a condescending tone and constantly interrupts you, and you want to set a boundary about how you prefer to be spoken to by this person going forward. This person can be a friend, a family member, a co-worker or a partner. I have a four-step plan for you to set a boundary effectively.

1. Identify what the behaviour is.
2. Say how it makes you feel.
3. Tell them what you would prefer them to do.
4. Tell them what will happen if they don't.

Say you're speaking to your partner here, it could be as simple as this: 'Excuse me, babe, but (1) when I speak and you continually interrupt me, (2) I feel annoyed and as if I'm not being listened to. (3) So going forward, when I speak, can you please let me finish what I am saying before responding so I feel respected, and (4) if you don't, I will simply no longer share my thoughts with you.'

This four-step boundary-setting exercise can be used in any type of relationship, and you can adjust the formality of the language and the type of request you're making accordingly.

If the idea of this conversation scares you, then I suggest it might be the opposite of what you learned growing up, and that you might be sacrificing your own well-being for the benefit of others. People who struggle with this especially struggle with the follow through on point 4, telling them what happens if they don't respect your boundary. The consequences you lay out here must be executed, because if you don't and your boundary gets violated again, this sets a precedent for people to ignore them altogether. Remember, their needs are not more important than your boundaries.

Exercise 2: The scorpion and the frog

This is a wonderful fable and a very applicable metaphor for the expectations of our relationships. A scorpion is walking through the jungle and arrives at a fast-flowing river. The scorpion sees a frog on the river bank and politely asks the frog for a lift across the river. The frog says, 'Absolutely not! You are a scorpion! You will sting me, and we will both drown.' The scorpion replies, 'No, I won't! I need to get across myself!' After some hesitation, the frog agrees and begins the journey across the river with the scorpion on his back. Halfway across the stream, the scorpion stings the frog, and they both begin to sink. The frog desperately asks, 'Why did you do that?!' and the scorpion responds, 'Because I'm a scorpion, of course.'

Do you see the point? Your expectations of people's behaviours are represented by the frog, wide eyed and naive, while the reality of their behaviour is the scorpion. Quite often our chronically late partner, who has never made it to any appointment on time their entire life, generates a negative emotional response when they are, inevitably, late to come meet us. But why are you so upset, little frog? Why allow that scorpion to get on your back? Accept that the lateness is who they are, and that if you expect them to be late from the beginning then you needn't be angry when they inevitably are.

Most of the time the frustration that we have with people's behaviours is that we expect them to behave in a way that they have never once shown themselves to be capable of. We romanticise a change in behaviour and pin our hopes to it, even if they have shown no inclination for this change. To be clear, I am not in any way suggesting you should allow a partner, friend, family member or colleague to disrespect you or abuse you, and this metaphor does not extend to grossly inappropriate and unacceptable behaviour. I am simply saying that, for the recurring annoyances we have of others, if you can instead accept who a person really is, flaws and all, then you needn't have an emotional response when they are exactly who they are.

Objective observation of people's behaviours will allow you to see true patterns and create the emotional space for yourself to not be surprised and frustrated by it. Next time you find yourself being frustrated and upset by a person's attitudes, behaviours and beliefs, ask yourself if you are being a frog expecting the scorpion not to sting. Ask yourself if you are not the architect of your own distress, simply by expecting them to behave a way that you would, or think that they should, or imagine that they will. The chances are that if you accept that everyone will do what they want in the time that they feel is right, then you needn't ever respond negatively to it. If you can accept that a person's behaviours are only ever a reflection of them and their perspectives, their attitudes, their conditioned behaviours and beliefs, then you needn't get angry. If their attitudes, behaviours or beliefs are an infringement on your boundaries, then re-establish those boundaries, and if they are not respected then step away from that person. But do all this, without losing your temper, without losing control. Their behaviours are their choices, it is not your responsibility to manage or fight against what they choose.

Summary

I would be nowhere near where I am today, and I would not perceive myself as successful, if it weren't for the brilliant people in my life. The support, the love, the patience, the kindness the discipline, the bollockings and the big dreaming that my friends and peers have offered me. I'm sure you feel the same. The Relationships pillar is built from the connections we have with the people around us, and without them our mental resilience will come crashing down.

The power of growing this resilience really comes through in my friendship groups and when I look for the boundaries I've set with people, and what is and isn't respected. I continuously check for genuine connections and assess why I feel a certain way about someone. The people who I surround myself with will either make or break my self-belief.

I challenge you to be authentic and open with the people around you and pursue what you want to achieve with great gusto and passion. If you do this, the right people will be drawn to you. The people who try to pull you down serve no purpose, especially if they do not respect your boundaries. You can forgive them, but you also have to move on. Accept these people as the scorpions that they are and you need never be a frog, stung by their behaviours. The relationships in your life will lead you to very brilliant or very dark places, so remember to put those boundaries in and strive to achieve your goals, and along the way help others succeed too. Release the egocentric idea of loneliness and solitude as the facilitators to success and fulfilment, and instead realise that it is in the right tribe that you will find the way not only to your fulfilment, but to everyone else's too.

We are stronger together.

CONCLUSION

There is a lot of information in this book. Having now finished almost all of it, you may find it daunting to start on your path to mental resilience. I often find that when I read a book, I like to boil it down to a few useful points, things to carry with me, things that have helped me form the perspective that has allowed me to write this book and develop the ideas within it. I will do the same for you.

Please note, of course, that after reading this book you will not instantly be the most mentally resilient human in the world. It simply doesn't work like that. Instead, I hope that it enables and empowers you to understand your emotions and learn how to manage them better. I hope it shows you how to handle stress, pressure, life, challenges and the pursuit of your subjective fulfilments. I truly hope that there might be something, even if it's just one thing, that you read in this entire book, that inspires a change, that makes you think or makes you challenge a set perspective that you previously held, and that it brings an element of control to that area of your life.

For these things to happen, you must be open to the idea of change. I was once trying to explain to someone how soldiers' brains are damaged from excessive trauma and the observable differences in it. To emphasise this, I showed the individual the opening chapter from the legendary book *The Body Keeps the Score* by Bessel van der Kolk. The opening chapter talks of his work in

sleep and how he went from there into the neuroscience of trauma.[1]
The said person read this extract, handed me the book back and
said in an extremely dismissive tone, 'I like how he looked into
sleep, that's the most important', and walked off.

This was upsetting – something I hold so dear was being
dismissed by someone, and it felt like a rejection of myself. This
is an accurate representation of how most people react when
presented with information that challenges their own perspective.
Most people don't like to be challenged, or when they are challenged, they simply hear what they want to hear. There are many
examples of this: a person telling me that their impatience is a
good thing, or the way someone brazenly speaks to people to get
what they want at any cost, or how they think that being openly
emotionally volatile, spilling their stress onto others, is an asset.
When challenged and told that maybe they don't see the entire
picture of how their behaviour comes across and perhaps need to
take a moment to consider other perspectives and the best way
forward, they don't want to hear it. Either someone has validated
this behaviour as good, or it is something they believe has helped
them survive up to now. People don't only cling onto helpful
behaviours, they're just as committed to keeping the attributes
that sabotage them.

Getting stuck in your own view of the world is not the way
forward. Being open to change instead means exactly what it says:
you need to open your mind to new perspectives and realise that
no matter how entrenched your beliefs are about yourself and
about how the world works, this perspective can shift. I hope this
book has helped you do this.

Whenever I finish reading a book, I check myself for my biases.
I make sure I have not heard only what I want to hear and not
twisted a piece of information out of context to fit my own narrative. I compare what I have read to what I previously thought to

be true and how willing I am to hear something different. I also note what has resonated with me and why. It is important that we ask these questions, otherwise we run the risk of only absorbing what we already believe anyway.

I remember a very astute quote from Agent K, played by the brilliant Tommy Lee Jones, in *Men in Black*: '1500 years ago, everybody "knew" the Earth was the centre of the universe; 500 years ago, everybody "knew"' the earth was flat. And 15 minutes ago, you "knew" that humans were alone on this planet. Imagine what you'll "know" tomorrow.' A wonderful geeky reference there. But it's true. Being open to new information, placing yourself at the altar of knowledge and acknowledging that you actually know very little is the best way to learn.

The conclusion of this book is this: a person can drown in a paddling pool, or a person can drown in an ocean. The size of the body of water is irrelevant, what matters is that someone is drowning and needs saving. You can dive in time and time again to save them, but you must teach them how to swim so that they can save themselves. And teaching someone to swim becomes a lot easier if you yourself have had to learn to swim.

We don't compare traumas, we don't belittle or invalidate ourselves. We identify the emotions that we feel, and we ask ourselves why. How can you ever manage yourself if you never learn to understand and appreciate the sources of your emotions? You accept those emotions, you reason with yourself and you breathe.

To repeat what I said early on in the book, resilience takes many forms and comparing your perception of your struggles to somebody else will do nothing but destroy your ability to be resilient. Never perceiving yourself as being capable enough to even start developing mental resilience is a great way of destroying your own ability to withstand any adversity, difficulty or challenge. It becomes a self-fulfilling prophecy.

The Five Pillars of Mental Resilience have been developed over years of trial and error. I used to switch my opinion of what they would look like constantly. I questioned whether I was teaching them right, what a condensed version would look like, what I could convey to people in a small amount of time, what that would look and feel like, how I could generate interest, if I was even right at all, and whether that mattered or not. What I have learned is that people are extremely subjective and nuanced and there may well be a person reading this book saying, 'This is brilliant!' and recommending it to all their friends, and someone else saying, 'This is awful!' and throwing the book in a charity bin or deleting it from their device.

But whatever your perspective, I hope you now have a significant toolbox to help manage your challenges. I hope you have a fairly all-encompassing method of what to do, how to do it and what that looks and feels like. I hope you now know how to acknowledge and accept your emotional state and how to deal with it effectively. I hope you understand what you can do when you find yourself emotionally overwhelmed and how to do it. And that is a true superpower. The ability to hold yourself together and continue to strive towards your goal with purpose and deliberation is a gift that not many people will master or effectively execute. But there is no reason why you cannot now use these skills in a context that suits you and why you cannot continue to use them and adapt and evolve them to your needs.

In case you feel any guilt about this, please don't. These tools are helpful in general, but being able to adapt them to fit your specific needs is absolutely the point. Even if it feels wrong to shift the focus to your own needs and put yourself first, you are allowed to look after yourself, in fact it is your prime objective. Who else will look after you if not you? And how will you look after others if you don't look after yourself? Remember any in-flight safety demonstration you've ever seen: you put your own oxygen mask on first before helping others with theirs.

We all have our own perspectives on and ideas about the world and I hope that there is one tool at least that you can take away, use and develop for your own needs and that it in some way provides you with relief or fortitude whenever you need it to.

For me, at the moment of writing this book I use my pillar of relationships a lot. As I navigate the world and grow and find my own niche and nuanced field, the people around me change. You might be lucky, like me with some of my old mates, to have some people in your life who will always be there, but I must remember that who I spend time with will naturally change.

I spent 14 years in the military, surrounded by my tribe of wonderful idiots who have taught me so much about who I am and what I'm capable of. And now I find myself sitting at a table in the scoff house of King's College London, with these incredibly educated, intelligent people discussing current events, soaking up their knowledge and expertise and brilliance. It's an entirely new world to me. When someone drops a cup in the canteen, I have to fight every instinct I have to not very loudly and belligerently shout, 'WWHEEEYYY!!' followed by a series of crow noises (military inside joke: a crow is an insult for a green recruit). I am sure that the various academically brilliant people wouldn't find this in the slightest bit amusing.

One phase ends, and a new one begins. I am now desperately trying to not say anything stupid that may out me as the fool I believe I am, anything that might indicate that I don't belong here, that I just got lost and ended up in the wrong place. None of this is true of course, but this is how we feel when we challenge ourselves and find ourselves in unfamiliar environments. We feel like an impostor.

One classmate, a particularly brilliant and educated woman, leans over to me and checks that I have had enough to eat. I assure her that I have, and she reminds me to take a little extra with me. I smile, I have built a strong pillar with her here for sure. She reminds me that I have to print off the cover sheet for my essay submission and that if I do it now I won't have to worry about it next week. She shows me how to do it, I get her a coffee as a thank you. It helps me feel safe and secure.

There are brilliant people everywhere, make sure that you find them.

There are times that I move between pillars depending on the situation that I face. I have become addicted to asking myself 'why'. For example, I am writing this in a very middle-class coffee shop. The people next to me are speaking too loudly and I'm annoyed. But why am I annoyed? Is it because they are speaking too loudly or simply because I am not being focused enough on my writing? After sitting on this for a while I decide on the latter, because this is something I actually control. I instantly think of FOCUS, from the Emotional Intelligence pillar, breathe and remember that, in a similar situation, I would tell my daughter Georgie to block out the noise and focus on what she needs to do. I pull my headphones on and find my liquid DnB (Drum and Bass with more melody) playlist and slip into study mode.

The pillars you need to focus on each time might change. Be open to that change and be flexible in your thinking. The world around you evolves. Evolve with it, and see change as an opportunity to perform. 'Chaos is a ladder,' said Littlefinger in *Game of Thrones*. Don't create chaos to trample on others though. Instead, perceive the situations that you find yourself in as opportunities to grow and learn and to set an example to others so that they too may see your development, growth and use of the pillars. Hopefully they will then say, 'I want that too!' and look up to you as an example to strive towards.

It is human to struggle, it is human to err. It is what bonds and binds us. It's an unspoken energy between us all – that none of us really knows anything for certain, that we cannot have faith that nothing will ever go wrong, that the only thing we can actually have true faith in is in our ability to cope. So be that example. In the infamous words of David Gilmour, Roger Waters and Richard Wright: 'Shine on you crazy diamond.'

Stronger, together, always.

A LETTER FROM JAMES

I want to say a huge for choosing to read my book *Think Yourself Resilient*. If you enjoyed it and want to keep updated with my latest activities, take a moment to sign up at the following link (your email address will never be shared, and you can unsubscribe at any time):

www.thread-books.com/sign-up

I didn't set out to write a book, I didn't even set out to speak to large groups of people. The plan was, and always will be, 'save one'. If I can make a difference to one person's life that potentially stops them from hurting themselves or worse, then brilliant. I am blessed to say that has already happened many times, and each time I always start the cognitive process again with 'save one'. The fact that people want to read or hear my words, consider them and bring positive change on themselves because of something I have said or written is still incredibly alien to me, but that doesn't mean that I am not incredibly thankful. It's very fulfilling for me to see that I have helped someone change their life for the better.

This book, from the first moment I started collecting my thoughts until I finished it, has been two years in the making. I have drawn so much from my personal experiences as a child growing up in a difficult family environment, as a lost teenager, a soldier, a father, a psychotherapist, a resilience coach and a human being who has struggled with mental health throughout my life.

I have found writing it to be therapeutic and sad and full of life and glee. I really hope that comes across for you, my reader.

I would be very grateful if you could write a review and help other readers discover this book and embark on the journey of becoming more resilient.

If you have questions about the book, challenges to the words, further exploration of ideas or simply want a chat, I am not a hard man to find on social media. I exist on both Instagram and LinkedIn. I await your response eagerly.

Thank you for your time reading this book. I hope that it helps and that you too may 'save one'.

Soft landings,
James

 @jameselliottofficial

 james-elliott

james-elliott.mykajabi.com

FURTHER READING

An academic book about how our lifestyle choices affect our health: Binns, A., Egger, G., Rossner, S. & Sagner M. (2017). *Lifestyle Medicine* (third edition). Cambridge, MA: Academic Press.

Habits expert on how small decisions can have life-altering outcomes: Clear, J. (2018). *Atomic Habits.* London: Random House Business.

A guide to physical development that will help you achieve your goals: Chadwick, M. (2022). *The Red On Revolution.* Leicester: W.F. Howes.

A book about the care system and the care experience: Cherry, L. (2022). *The Brightness of Stars.* London: Routledge.

Dr Frankl's revolutionary logotherapy approach: Frankl, V. (2004). *Man's Search for Meaning.* London: Rider.

A classic, offering insight and advice about overcoming our fears: Jeffers, S. (2012). *Feel The Fear And Do It Anyway.* London: Vermillion.

A book on how the human mind makes decisions and how people's judgement can be improved: Lehrer, J. (2009). *The Decisive Moment.* Edinburgh: Canongate Books.

A book about the science behind why humans behave as they do: Sapolsky, R. (2018). *Behave*. London: Vintage.

A book about tackling life's everyday ups and downs: Smith, J. (2022). *Why Has Nobody Told Me This Before?* London: Michael Joseph.

A book exploring trauma in depth: van der Kolk, B. (2014). *The Body Keeps the Score*. London: Viking.

ACKNOWLEDGEMENTS

I would like to thank the Thread team for having faith in me. They probably doubted their decision to publish me more than once when I turned up with holes in my jeans and coffee spilled down my shirt, or when I hadn't written enough. I obviously wouldn't have made it here without you, especially my editors Alba Proko and Nina Winters, who both deserve a month's holiday and a pay rise.

To those I love, to Robert Amos and Kate Amos, thank you for everything. To Witney RFC, Aldo and JC, and big shout out to the green shed. Thank you, Colchester RFC, you became a home for me and a bastion of strength when I needed it most.

To the British Army and the fantastic people who make it brilliant. I miss you monkeys, but I do not miss the circus. That being said, I'd give it all up in a heartbeat to be back in P troop (the preparatory training troop, especially for aspiring young potential airborne recruits) running around in the mud.

Soaps, Swede, Mrs Swede, Carl, Mrs Jordan, Marshy (such a great little guy) and the Chi-Chis, who have told me off, laughed and cried with me, fed, entertained and supported me, despite my many many faults and failings. I believe it is my turn to get the brews on.

ENDNOTES

What is Mental Resilience?

1. Snowden, R. (2006). *Freud: The Key Ideas*. London: Teach Yourself.
2. Ekman, P. (1992). 'Are there basic emotions?' *Psychological Review*, 99, 550–553. Washington: American Psychological Association. Available from: https://psycnet.apa.org/doiLanding?doi=10.1037%2F0033-295X.99.3.550.

Preparing the Ground

1. Kishimi, I. & Koga, F. (2013). *The Courage to be Disliked*. Crows Nest, New South Wales: Allen & Unwin Books.

Chapter One: Confidence

1. Citizens Advice. (2021). Three million families facing crisis as cost of living crunch bites. Available from: www.citizensadvice.org.uk/about-us/about-us1/media/press-releases/three-million-families-facing-crisis-as-cost-of-living-crunch-bites.
2. Bywaters, P. *et al.* (2016). 'The relationship between poverty, child abuse and neglect: An evidence review.' Joseph Rowntree Foundation. Available from: www.jrf.org.

uk/report/relationship-between-poverty-child-abuse-and-neglect-evidence-review.

3. Sparrow, A. (2022). 'More than half of UK's black children live in poverty, analysis shows.' *The Guardian*. Available from: www.theguardian.com/world/2022/jan/02/more-than-half-of-uks-black-children-live-in-poverty-analysis-shows.

4. Mohr, T.S. (2014). 'Why women don't apply for jobs unless they're 100% qualified.' *Harvard Business Review*. Available from: https://hbr.org/2014/08/why-women-dont-apply-for-jobs-unless-theyre-100-qualified.

5. Kishimi, I. & Koga, F. (2013). *The Courage to be Disliked*. Crows Nest, New South Wales: Allen & Unwin Books.

6. Bowlby, J. (1958). 'The nature of the child's tie to his mother.' *The International Journal of Psychoanalysis*, 39, 350–371. Washington: American Psychological Association. Available from: https://psycnet.apa.org/record/1960-02815-001

7. Kirk, I. (2022). 'How many Britons display signs of impostor syndrome?' *YouGov*. Available from: https://yougov.co.uk/topics/society/articles-reports/2022/06/07/how-many-britons-display-signs-impostor-syndrome.

Chapter Two: Emotional Intelligence

1. Bouchard, T. *et al.* (1990). 'Sources of human psychological differences: The Minnesota study of twins reared apart.' *Science*, 250(4978), 223–228. Available from: www.science.org/doi/10.1126/science.2218526.

2. Sun, T. (2004). 'Logic vs emotion: And the winner Is?' *Columbus Business First*. Available from: www.bizjournals.com/columbus/stories/2004/11/01/smallb2.html.

3. Keltner, D. *et al.* (2019).'Emotional expression: Advances in basic emotion theory.' *Journal of Nonverbal Behavior*, 42(2), 133–160. Available from: www.ncbi.nlm.nih.gov/pmc/articles/PMC6687086.
4. van der Kolk, B. (2014). *The Body Keeps the Score*. London: Viking.

Chapter Three: Physical Health

1. van der Kolk, B. (2014). *The Body Keeps the Score*. London: Viking.
2. Griffiths, R. (2019). *Depression: The Mind-Body, Diet and Lifestyle Connection*. New York, NY: Clink Street Publishing.
3. Hensel, D.J. *et al.* (2016). 'The association between sexual health and physical, mental, and social health in adolescent women.' *Journal of Adolescent Health*, 59(4), 416–421. Available from: https://pubmed.ncbi.nlm.nih.gov/27491340.
4. Heider, F. (1958). *The Psychology of Interpersonal Relations*. Eastford, CT: Martino Fine Books.

Chapter Four: Goals

1. Meijer, E. *et al.* (2018). 'Identity processes in smokers who want to quit smoking: A longitudinal interpretative phenomenological analysis'. *Health: An Interdisciplinary Journal for the Social Study of Health, Illness and Medicine*, 24(5). Available from: https://journals.sagepub.com/doi/10.1177/1363459318817923.
2. Clear, J. (2018). *Atomic Habits*. London: Random House Business.
3. Frankl, V. (2004). *Man's Search for Meaning*. London: Rider.

4. Sinek, S. (2009). *Start With Why*. London: Portfolio.
5. Macaulay, T.B. (1846). *Lays of Ancient Rome*. London: Longman.
6. Sapolsky, R. (2018). *Behave*. London: Vintage.

Chapter Five: Relationships

1. Solms, M. (2002). *An Introduction to the Neuroscientific Works of Sigmund Freud*. London: Routledge.
2. Holt-Lunstad, J, *et al.* (2015). 'Loneliness and social isolation as risk factors for mortality: A meta-analytic review.' *Perspectives on Psychological Science*, 10(1). Available from: https://journals.sagepub.com/doi/abs/10.1177/1745691614568352.
3. Gov.UK. (2018). 'PM launches Government's first loneliness strategy.' Available from: www.gov.uk/government/news/pm-launches-governments-first-loneliness-strategy.
4. Umberson, D. & Karas Montez, J. (2010). 'Social relationships and health: A flashpoint for health policy.' *Journal of Health and Social Behavior*, 51, 54–66. Available from: www.ncbi.nlm.nih.gov/pmc/articles/PMC3150158.
5. Shaw, K. (2014). 'How your brain decides who to make friends with when you start university.' *The Conversation*. Available from: https://theconversation.com/how-your-brain-decides-who-to-make-friends-with-when-you-start-university-32306.

Conclusion

1. van der Kolk, B. (2014). *The Body Keeps the Score*. London: Viking.